SOLVING MEDICARE PROBLEM$

Steve Forbes,
Let's work together
to change the
tax system!
 Woodrow Wilkins

SOLVING MEDICARE PROBLEM$

An Introduction for Beginners

By
Woodrow Wilcox

E-BookTime, LLC
Montgomery, Alabama

Solving Medicare Problem$
An Introduction for Beginners

Copyright © 2012 by Woodrow Wilcox

Articles copyrighted © 2003 through 2012 by Woodrow Wilcox

All rights reserved. No part of this book may be reproduced or transmitted in any form or by any means, electronic or mechanical, including photocopying, recording, or by any information storage and retrieval system, without permission in writing from the copyright owner.

DISCLAIMER: Laws, regulations, rules, and procedures change. The author is not a lawyer and does not give legal advice. The contents of this book are for informational purposes only. Contact the legal advisor of your choice for any legal questions.

Library of Congress Control Number: 2012947767

ISBN: 978-1-60862-426-3

First Edition
Published September 2012
E-BookTime, LLC
6598 Pumpkin Road
Montgomery, AL 36108
www.e-booktime.com

Contents

PREFACE 11

INTRODUCTION 13
    WHO SHOULD BUY THIS BOOK? 13
    WHO WROTE THIS BOOK? 13

CHAPTER ONE *HELPING SENIOR CITIZENS BY SOLVING MEDICARE PROBLEMS* 15
    HOW IT BEGAN 15
    HOW SERIOUS IS THE PROBLEM? 18
    WHO SHOULD STUDY THIS MATERIAL? 19

CHAPTER TWO *IT'S ALL ABOUT HELPING SENIOR CITIZENS WHO NEED HELP* 21
    IMAGINE BEING A SENIOR CITIZEN WITH A MEDICARE MEDICAL BILL PROBLEM 21
    IMAGINE HOW YOU WILL FEEL AFTER HELPING SENIOR CITIZENS 22
    SOME ARTICLES THAT WILL HELP YOU TO UNDERSTAND THE NEED 24
    SAVED WIDOW ALMOST $400 24
    CLIENT FELT BETTER AFTER VISIT 25
    WIDOWER WORRIED BY $1100 BILL 26
    VIDEO CLIP HELPS SAVE SENIOR CITIZEN 27

CHAPTER THREE *LEARN THE "NUTS AND BOLTS" OF THE MEDICARE SYSTEM* 29
    HOW DOES THE MEDICARE SYSTEM WORK? 29
    OUTLINE OF TALK BY WOODROW WILCOX AT KNIGHTS OF COLUMBUS (COUNCIL # 4047) IN MERRILLVILLE INDIANA 30
    BEWARE OF DIFFERENT RULES FOR DIFFERENT PARTS OF MEDICARE 32
    MEDICARE MECHANICS 33
    TECHNICAL MEDICARE MATTERS 34
    DON'T DISCARD MEDICARE SUMMARY NOTICE 36
    MEDICARE DOESN'T COVER EVERYTHING 37
    DOCTOR'S OFFICE FILED CLAIM INCORRECTLY 39

A DISADVANTAGE TO MEDICARE ADVANTAGE
POLICIES 40

CHAPTER FOUR *THREE TYPES OF PROBLEMS* 43
    TYPE ONE: POLICY PROBLEMS 43
    TYPE TWO: HUMAN ERROR PROBLEMS 43
    MEDICARE MISTAKE "KILLED" SENIOR 44
    MISTAKES HAPPEN – GIVE PEOPLE A CHANCE TO
    CORRECT MISTAKES 45
    PROTECTING CLIENTS/PATIENTS FROM BILLING
    MISTAKES OR FRAUD 46
    THE HOSPITAL LIED 47
    TYPE THREE: TECHNOLOGY CAUSED PROBLEMS 48

CHAPTER FIVE *ARTICLES WITH A POINT* 50
    LEARN AND FOLLOW MEDICARE RULES TO
    SAVE MONEY 50
    MAKE SURE OLD INSURANCE COMPANY GOT
    CANCELLATION LETTER 51
    AVOIDING INSURANCE PROBLEMS AFTER YOU QUIT
    WORKING WHILE ON MEDICARE 52
    WHEN SENIORS TRAVEL OUTSIDE THE U.S.A. 53
    DELAYED FILING CAN CAUSE PROBLEMS 55
    NOTIFY INSURANCE COMPANY OF CLIENT DEATH
    PROMPTLY 56
    DON'T BLAME INSURANCE AGENT OR COMPANY
    WHEN MEDICARE MAKES MISTAKES! 56
    ADVANTAGES OF USING A LOCAL INSURANCE AGENT 58
    HOW TO USE INSURANCE AGENCIES AND INSURANCE
    COMPANIES BETTER 59
    SAVED MICHIGAN CITY MAN $815 61
    MEDICARE AS PRIMARY INSURER VERSUS MEDICARE
    AS SECONDARY INSURER 61
    SWITCHING MEDICARE SUPPLEMENT POLICIES
    TAKES TIME 62
    MEDICARE UPDATE OVER SIX MONTHS BEHIND 64
    SAVED RETIRED TEACHER HUNDREDS 66
    CHESTERTON WOMAN FORGOT ABOUT ANNUAL
    DEDUCTIBLE 67

SAVED MERRILLVILLE WOMAN $510 68
EXPENSIVE AMBULANCE RIDE 69
CLIENT SIGNED AGREEMENT TO PAY MORE THAN
MEDICARE APPROVED 70
HOSPITAL AND MEDICARE DATA DID NOT MATCH 71
HOSPITAL DEMANDED OVER $2,000 AFTER BILL WAS
ALREADY PAID 71
BAD ADVICE FROM ADULT CHILDREN HARMED
MOTHER 72

CHAPTER SIX *WORKING THROUGH THE PROBLEM* 74
SAVE THE PAPERWORK! 76

CHAPTER SEVEN *EXAMPLE LETTERS* 80
LETTERS FROM AGENCY/AGENT TO CLIENT/PATIENT 81
    LETTER TO CLIENT TO ANSWER QUESTION
    ABOUT COVERAGE 81
    LETTER TO CLIENT ABOUT MISSING INFORMATION ... 82
    ANOTHER LETTER TO A CLIENT ABOUT NEED FOR
    MEDICARE SUMMARY NOTICE FORM 83
    LETTER TO CLIENT TO EXPLAIN ANNUAL
    DEDUCTIBLE 84
    LETTER TO CLIENT TO REDUCE WORRY 85
    LETTER TO CLIENT ABOUT CHARGES
    DISALLOWED BY MEDICARE 85
    LETTER TO CLIENT ABOUT HEARING AID 86
    LETTER TO CLIENT ABOUT ANNUAL DEDUCTIBLES ... 87
    LETTER TO CLIENT RE: DISALLOWED X-RAY
    CHARGES 88
    LETTER TO CLIENT RE: $500 BILL 89
    FOLLOW UP LETTER AFTER CLIENT RESPONSE 90
    LETTER ABOUT MSN PAGE ONE MISSING 91
    LETTER TO CLIENT REGARDING EYE CLINIC BILL 92
    LETTER TO CLIENT – NEED OLD BILL INFO 93
    LETTER TO GIVE CLIENT GOOD NEWS 94
    LETTER TO CLIENT RE: MISSING PAGE OF MSN
    AND LETTERS 95

Contents

LETTERS FROM CLIENT/PATIENT TO THIRD PARTIES.........96
    LETTER TO MEDICAL SERVICE PROVIDER......................97
    LETTER FOR CLIENT TO SIGN FOR FIXING
    MEDICARE PART D PROBLEM..98
    LETTER TO MEDICAL SERVICE PROVIDER RE:
    TWO INSURANCE COMPANIES AND CLAIMS.................99
    LETTER TO MEDICAL SERVICE PROVIDER WHEN
    INFORMATION ABSENT...101
    LETTER TO MEDICAL CLINIC RE: THREE
    BALANCES...102
    LETTER ABOUT TWO PROBLEMS WITH BILL.............103
    LETTER TO MEDICAL OFFICE TO HELP CLIENT
    WITH BILL PROBLEM..104
    LETTER TYPED FOR CLIENT TO CORRECT
    HOSPITAL BILLING RECORDS...106
    LETTER TYPED FOR CLIENT TO SEND TO
    MEDICARE..107
    LETTER TO HOSPITAL RE: MEDICARE SKEWED
    NUMBERS..108
    LETTER TO HOSPITAL RE: $480 BILL...............................109
    LETTER TO ADVISE OF BILLING ERRORS....................110
    LETTER TO HOSPITAL TO REVIEW AND
    CORRECT BILL..111
    LETTER TO HOSPITAL TO CORRECT BILL
    TO ZERO..112
    LETTER FOR CLIENT TO SEND TO MEDICAL
    SERVICE PROVIDER..113
    LETTER TO CREDITOR AND COLLECTION
    LAW FIRM...115
    LETTER ABOUT NO RECORD OF CLAIM.......................116

CHAPTER EIGHT *MORE ARTICLES FOR GREATER
UNDERSTANDING*..118
    THREE HOURS FOR ONE CLIENT.....................................118
    ASK FOR HELP WITH VA-MEDICARE PROBLEMS.......119
    SAVED HIGHLAND WOMAN OVER $2500.....................120
    WORKING WITH AN ANGRY DAUGHTER.....................121
    SURPRISE MEDICARE RULING COSTS SENIOR...........122
    ACCIDENTS AND MEDICARE CLAIMS...........................123

Contents

UNREALISTIC RULES AND REGULATIONS 124
NICE THANK YOU NOTE 125
NICE APOLOGY FROM HOSPITAL 126
SAVED CROWN POINT WOMAN $1100 126
THREE BILLS IN ONE MONTH 127
HOSPITAL DOUBLE BILLED CLIENT 128
BILL INFO DID NOT MATCH 129
SAVED HIGHLAND WOMAN $345 130
SAVED CEDAR LAKE MAN OVER $500 131
BEE STING AND BILL STING 132
MEDICARE MAKING "PIDDLY" WORK 133
MEDICARE LOST 2 OF 3 CLAIMS 134
MEDICARE REFUSED BREAST AND PELVIC EXAMS 135
PRIVATE ENTERPRISE MOVES FASTER 136
MEDICARE RECORDS UPDATE SLOW 136
HELPING AN UPSET VETERAN 137
PAID BILL SENT TO COLLECTION 139
CHINESE AMERICAN CLIENT HAD A QUESTION 140
MEDICARE 18 MONTHS PAST DUE 141
ANOTHER TYPICAL DAY 142
MEDICARE IS A COMPLICATED SYSTEM 143

CHAPTER NINE *SELF-ADMINISTERED DRUGS* 144
   THE "SELF-ADMINISTERED DRUG" PROBLEM
   EXPLAINED 144
   THE PROBLEM OF "SELF-ADMINISTERED DRUGS" 147
   HELP WITH "SELF-ADMINISTERED DRUGS" 148

CHAPTER TEN *FUTURE PROBLEMS FROM "OBAMACARE"* 151
   MEDICARE MAKING PROBLEMS FOR BOTH
   DOCTORS AND PATIENTS 153
   EYE DOCTORS COMPLAIN ABOUT MEDICARE 154
   FEDERAL MEDICARE BUREAUCRATS REFUSED TO
   PAY BILL 155
   MEDICARE REFUSED TO PAY FOR X-RAY OF
   LOWELL MAN 156
   A PAINFUL BEGINNING FOR HEALTH CARE REFORM 157
   "OBAMACARE" TV NEWS INTERVIEW 159

Contents

COUSIN IKE'S WARNING 160
MY GRANDMA AND MY PROFESSOR 164

CHAPTER ELEVEN *WRITING ARTICLES ABOUT SOLVING MEDICARE PROBLEMS* 166

CHAPTER TWELVE *FINAL THOUGHTS* 169

PREFACE

I think for myself. If something does not make sense to me, I search for an alternative that does make sense. Sometimes, that puts me at odds with others.

Some people may not like this book. Some people may not like the way that I wrote this book. That's their problem.

There are at least three items about this book in which I have gone "against the grain". So, don't blame the publisher or an editor. I did it. It was my decision.

The first area is the matter of punctuation with commas. I believe that commas should be used wherever a speaker would pause briefly. Communication with language is not just the words. Much of communication is outside or around the words. People learn language skills in this order: listening, speaking, reading, writing. The writing should help to present the material as though someone were speaking to the reader. Commas help to express the material in this way. I know that some people want to reduce the number of commas and other word tools used for the sake of economy of words or space. But, many times, I have been frustrated to have to read something twice and then I realized that the reason for the need to read it twice was because the item read was not well punctuated and was confusing for a lack of punctuation. So, I use commas whenever and wherever I believe it reflects where I would pause briefly if I were talking and reading to you from this book.

The second area is in the difference between the *American rule* and the *British rule* regarding the use of quotation marks, especially at the end of sentences. The *American rule* regularly places punctuation inside quotation marks. The British rule places punctuation marks inside the quote only if the punctuation is actually a part of the quote as in a period at the end of a sentence which is being quoted. Placing the punctuation inside the quotes under the American rule is fine when a person who is speaking is quoted, but not good when a document, story, or other writing is quoted.

The *British rule* makes much more sense since it distinguishes that which is being quoted more precisely. After all, why would it make sense to place within quotation marks a bit of punctuation which does not appear in the words or item being quoted? It seems to me that doing so could lead to a misunderstanding of the meaning or point which a writer or editor is attempting to make. So, in this book, I preferred to follow the *British rule*.

The third area is my choice of discussing one matter more than once. This annoys some people who want me to make a point once and then move to another point. But, I believe that repetition is a foundation of education and the purpose of this book is to educate. I believe that if you look at an object from several sides, you will have a better knowledge and appreciation of that object. Likewise, I believe that presenting similar problems from various angles will help the reader to have a better knowledge and appreciation of the subject discussed. Also, if I discuss a problem only once, the reader might think that the problem is not common. But, if I discuss the same or almost the same problem with a different client, the reader will find it easier to believe that the problem is common.

This is my book and I did it my way. Maybe I was inspired by a song by Frank Sinatra.

I have heard that lemmings are animals with such a strong herd instinct that they would follow a leader lemming over a cliff in droves. I don't know if that is true. I doubt it. But, if it is true and if I were a lemming, I believe that I would be one that would run away from the cliff because what the leader would be doing would make no sense to me.

What some leaders do makes no sense to me. So, I don't follow those leaders. I think for myself.

INTRODUCTION

WHO SHOULD BUY THIS BOOK?

- Attorneys who want to build their practice among senior citizens with a free or small charge service that will enhance their reputation and build their law practice with future business.
- Life and Health insurance agents who want to help senior citizens in their community and build a reputation that will bring more insurance business.
- Clergy and leaders of congregations who want to help the senior citizens in their respective congregations or help senior citizens in the community as an outreach ministry.
- Community leaders and officials who want to help senior citizens in their communities.
- Parish nurses of various churches and worship centers.
- Journalists who are not working for a news organization but who want to keep researching and writing while they wait for their next news position.
- Adults with senior citizen parents whom they want to protect from wrongful or erroneous medical bill charges.

* * * * * * * *

WHO WROTE THIS BOOK?

For over nine years, Woodrow Wilcox has served as the senior medical bill case worker at a large senior citizen oriented insurance agency in the Midwest. In seven and a half years, he helped the clients of that insurance agency to cancel over one million dollars of mistaken or wrongful medical bill charges that were caused by mistakes and faults in the Medicare system.

Woodrow Wilcox estimates that federal Medicare system caused wrongful charges cost senior citizens throughout America OVER ONE BILLION DOLLARS PER YEAR (on just Medicare Part A and Part B claims). Woodrow Wilcox wrote this book to encourage and help others to start helping senior citizens in other parts of the country.

Are you a person who wants to help senior citizens with Medicare medical bill problems in order to save money and aggravation for senior citizens? If you are, then this book is for you!

CHAPTER ONE

HELPING SENIOR CITIZENS BY SOLVING MEDICARE PROBLEMS

I have helped senior citizens to solve Medicare related medical bill problems for over nine years. I started in April 2003. In October 2010, I passed the one million dollar mark. That is to say that in seven and a half years, I saved senior citizens over one million dollars in Medicare related medical bill charges that they would have had to pay if I had not helped them to fix their problems.

* * * * * * * *

HOW IT BEGAN

When my mother retired from teaching, one insurance agent kept visiting her and asking for her business with a Medicare supplement insurance policy. One day when the insurance agent was visiting my mother on her front lawn, I arrived. She asked me if I thought that she should do business with this agent. I asked her how many other agents had asked her for her business in Medicare supplement insurance. She answered none.

So, I suggested that she do business with the visiting agent who was Fahed "Fred" Ulayyet. Fred Ulayyet remembered me for that and one other reason. I was one of the few Americans that he had met who spoke some Arabic.

Years later, I asked Fred Ulayyet to do me a favor and read an article that I wrote and was planning to publish on the internet. The article was

"Stop the Israel – Palestine Conflict with a 'Kentucky Solution'!" He liked the article and complimented me on it.

A few weeks after that, Fred Ulayyet asked me to answer the phones at his office for one day while his receptionist visited a doctor. While answering the phones, I learned from senior citizens that Medicare or their insurance companies were not paying some bills. I asked Fred Ulayyet about that. He told me what he knew of it and how he tried to help them.

Suddenly, everything clicked for me. I understood. It was easy for me to find the problem. I seemed to have a talent for finding the problems with medical bills that were not getting paid by Medicare or insurance companies.

Fred realized that I had this talent, too. A month later, after my one day of service, he asked me to come to work for his insurance agency full time. One of my areas of responsibility would be to help his senior citizen clients with their Medicare medical bill problems. This freed his time to do what he does best – which is meet people and sell insurance policies.

I did not take a course on how to help senior citizens with Medicare related medical bill problems. I simply learned while helping. As far as I know, Medicare does not offer a seminar or webinar on *how to fix a medical bill problem when Medicare makes a mistake.* Most government officials or employees don't want to admit that government makes a mistake about anything. In the entire time that I have worked at my friend's insurance agency, I never saw any mail that promoted a seminar for agents or agency staff on how to help senior citizen clients when medical bills were goofed by mistakes in the Medicare system. I never got any "official" training in this area. I simply helped senior citizens by interviewing, investigating, and thinking of solutions. So, I cannot and I do not cite federal Medicare statutes or regulations in this book to explain what I do. I believe that makes this publication more practical for most people.

One publication in which Fred Ulayyet's insurance agency bought advertising told him that he bought enough advertising space that he could submit an article to be published. Fred asked me to write the article. After the article was published in the northwest Indiana edition of *SENIOR LIFE*, other publications contacted me to ask if they could use the same article because they believed it was a good article for senior citizens. Mark Beall of *TV View* of northwest Indiana was the first of these other publishers to ask for permission to use the same article.

Then, I got the idea that I should contact other publications to offer to let them use my articles. The series of articles became a column by me about senior citizen issues. The articles are used mostly by publications based in Indiana and Illinois. But, sometimes up to 30 publications in 8 states have used my articles. I wrote the articles to help senior citizens who were not clients of the agency where I worked and to help attract new clients to my friend's insurance agency.

You can find many of these articles at www.woodrowwilcox.com and www.medicareproblems.net. Another publication that has many of my articles online is www.americanclarion.com but you must search "Woodrow Wilcox" at that website. Before, during, and after your study of this book, I suggest that you read articles on Medicare problems at these websites.

Some people learn better by reading an outline and some people learn better by reading stories. My articles at these sites are mostly stories of actual cases in which I have helped senior citizens. Anyone can read these stories *for free* at the websites. I have included some stories in this book, but not many. I have written over 300 stories about Medicare medical bill problems. If I included all the Medicare medical bill problem stories that I have written in this book, it might be too large a book for anyone to buy or bother to read. So, if you learn better by reading stories, do use the articles at these websites to augment your study of the material in this book.

The material in this book is not everything that I know about Medicare medical bill problems. This book does not have every possible solution or every solution that I have developed. It is written to be basic information that most people can understand and use to help with most (70 to 90 percent) Medicare medical bill problems.

A friend who is an attorney asked me how long it takes to work on each matter for a senior citizen. That varies. Usually, it takes about an hour to gather and review the papers or facts, and then write a letter or two to get the problem resolved. But, when an insurance company or Medicare must be phoned, the time is lengthened by the waiting while *on hold*. I have spent three hours or more on a single client. Also, I remember spending two hours in each of two sessions with a couple who had multiple problems. Sometimes, a senior citizen wants to talk more than what is needed to resolve the problem. In such a case, a gentle and polite reminder that I need to get to work to help other people with their problems ends our meeting nicely.

* * * * * * * *

HOW SERIOUS IS THE PROBLEM?

A few years ago, I wondered about the size and significance of the problem of Medicare medical bill mess-ups. I calculated how much I had saved our clients in an average week. I estimated what percentage of senior citizens in our congressional district were and were not our clients to find what should be a reasonable estimate of the problem for one congressional district. Then, I multiplied by the number of congressional districts. *The math resulted in an estimate that senior citizens around the U.S.A. are hit with over one billion dollars per year in wrongful medical bill charges which are caused by mistakes and problems in the Medicare system.* But, wait! That's not all! This one billion dollars per year estimate is for Medicare Part A and Part B problems alone. Medicare Part C and Medicare Part D generate more problems for senior citizens.

About the time that I did this calculation, James Flack, a friend of mine from Indianapolis, told me, "Woody, I think that you might be the only person in the country who is doing this for senior citizens. I haven't heard of anyone else doing this. It is unfortunate that others are not helping senior citizens in the same way."

It was a great compliment. But, I want my friend Fred Ulayyet to get credit for caring about his senior citizen clients enough to hire me to help them after he realized that I could do that and help both his clients and his business.

The statement of my friend from Indianapolis made me start to wonder how I could teach other people to do what I do to help senior citizens throughout America. Maybe by teaching other people what I do, I could help save thousands of senior citizens millions of dollars every year. If I could teach enough people to help save senior citizens 75 percent of wrongful Medicare related medical bill charges, then that would be like saving senior citizens around the country $750,000,000 each year. That would be great!

I made some drafts of some materials. My friend Sandra Pitzer arranged for me to test my materials with some of her friends at The First United Lutheran Church in Hammond, Indiana. I had a wonderful time with Sandra's church friends. They asked questions and helped me to refine my ideas and wording.

An acquaintance of mine at the National Religious Broadcasters (NRB) satellite channel in Nashville encouraged me to explore my idea of letting church clergy and congregation leaders learn what I do so that they can help the senior citizens in their churches or communities. If a clergy member or congregation leader can help the senior citizens in the congregation to save money, then, those senior citizens would be able to support the congregation with donations more easily.

You might be wondering that if this is such a big problem, why haven't you heard of it before *now*? Good question. I believe that several reasons combine to cause this.

- Many senior citizens simply send a check when a bill comes and don't question it.
- Many senior citizens don't know how to spot a problem with a medical bill. So, they pay a bill with a mistake without ever questioning it.
- Many insurance agents never were trained to read bills for mistakes because their job is to sell insurance – not to be the claims or customer service representative. But, insurance agents understand insurance terms and language which may confuse a senior citizen client. Also, insurance agents usually have the phone and fax lines needed to send and receive copies of forms that may relate to the problem. Insurance agents have special contracts with insurance companies for this.
- In my experience, hospitals, medical offices, laboratories, collection agencies, collection attorneys and Medicare do not take the initiative to help senior citizens with Medicare related medical bill problems.
- Some of the problems are very time consuming to fix. Senior citizens may give up in frustration. People who may try to help may give up in frustration, too.

* * * * * * * *

WHO SHOULD STUDY THIS MATERIAL?

I firmly believe that the best people to learn this material are **life and health insurance agents and their support staff members**. If they serve any senior citizens, then this book will help the agents to serve their senior citizen clients better.

But, I believe that other groups of people might be good for helping senior citizens, too. Attorneys who want to build a practice in senior citizen law can use this book to effectively offer free or small charge services to seniors in order to bring more business to their law practices. In a small community, someone in a town clerk's office could learn this material and help senior citizens of the town with their Medicare medical bill problems. Leaders of churches and other worship centers could learn this material so that they can help senior citizens in their congregations or senior citizens in their communities as an outreach ministry.

The main advantage that life and health insurance agents have over others is their familiarity with insurance language, practices, and procedures. There are certain federal laws which guard the privacy of people's healthcare and personal identity information which must be observed. Also, rules will change in the future and insurance agents are more likely to be notified of the changes earlier than most people.

When a senior citizen is not well physically or mentally, a *power of attorney* or other legal document is needed to help a senior citizen with a Medicare medical bill problem.

But, if a senior citizen is not incapacitated and can sit with another person who wants to help to solve a Medicare medical bill problem, then most problems can be solved without the need of a written power of attorney or limited power of attorney. The tools needed would be a telephone (preferably with a speaker phone option), a computer for typing, and a fax machine to fax documents when needed. I estimate that 70% to 90% of Medicare medical bill problems are simple enough to solve by people who are not attorneys.

I believe that if a person has those tools and has a good understanding of the system and how to find and resolve problems in Medicare medical billing, then helping a senior citizen in this matter can be accomplished rather easily.

Before you can help a senior citizen with a Medicare medical bill problem, you need to learn the basics of the Medicare system. That is what this book is designed to teach you: (1) How the system works; (2) How to find and resolve the problems; (3) Model letters and forms. Of course, you should read the publication from the *CENTERS FOR MEDICARE & MEDICAID SERVICES* entitled *"Choosing a Medigap Policy"*.

This book does not cover every possible problem. Medicare laws and regulations change and that will cause new problems to solve. But, this book does give a good foundation for resolving most problems that arise from errors and faults in the Medicare system.

CHAPTER TWO

IT'S ALL ABOUT HELPING SENIOR CITIZENS WHO NEED HELP

An old Native American Indian proverb advises that one should not criticize another until imagining what it is like to walk a mile in the other person's moccasins. So, let's imagine a bit.

* * * * * * * *

IMAGINE BEING A SENIOR CITIZEN WITH A MEDICARE MEDICAL BILL PROBLEM

Imagine yourself as a senior citizen. You are on a fixed income. You are on a tight budget. You do what you believe that you should do. You enroll in Medicare. You buy a Medicare supplement insurance policy. Then, you get some medical services and a big bill comes to you.

"Why didn't Medicare or the Medicare supplement insurance policy pay for this?" you wonder. Maybe your hearing is not as good as it used to be. Maybe your eyesight is not as good as it used to be. You call your insurance company or Medicare. But, something causes you frustration. You are put on "hold" for a long time. You accidentally press the wrong button in answer to a question and you wonder if you should start over with another phone call. The person who answers speaks with a thick foreign accent or does not speak loud enough for you to hear. You don't understand a question because it is in Medicare or medical insurance language which you don't understand. You can't find a form or a place on a form that the person on the other end of the line wants you to read so that a point can be clarified about your problem.

Senior citizens in this type of situation could use some help. If you are the kind of person who would like to help a senior citizen in such a situation, then you are reading something that can open that opportunity to you.

Helping senior citizens with such problems is often time consuming. *The work itself is not profitable.* By that I mean that it would be difficult or impossible to make a living on just helping with these problems because it is time consuming and most senior citizens couldn't afford to pay for such help. So, the help must come from someone who wants to help and hopes to profit from good feelings or good reputation which will bring rewards in other ways.

* * * * * * * *

IMAGINE HOW YOU WILL FEEL AFTER HELPING SENIOR CITIZENS

Relax. Breathe a deep breath. Now, imagine how you will feel after you help a senior citizen to correct a Medicare caused medical bill problem that saves the senior citizen hundreds or thousands of dollars. Imagine this. How do you feel? How does being helpful to the senior citizen feel to you? Hold that feeling. Then, think about how appreciative the senior citizen must be. Think about the relief that you helped that senior citizen to feel. You lifted a financial burden off the shoulders of that senior citizen. You eliminated a problem and worry for the senior citizen.

You will not accomplish this task or feel this satisfaction because of your good looks and great charm. You will experience this because you made the effort to learn how to read documents, ask questions, spot a problem, and devise a solution for a Medicare medical bill problem.

Following here is a partial list of some of the titles of articles that I wrote after helping a senior citizen. This is not a list of all the articles that I have written. By my last count, I had written over 300 Medicare problems articles. Note that I usually write only articles about simple problems that can be explained in a few paragraphs. I rarely write about the complex problems that I work to resolve. The articles would be too long and most readers and newspaper editors would be lost by the length or technical jargon.

Read the article titles on this list and then ask yourself if you are the type of person who would really want to do this work and enjoy this sometimes frustrating problem solving.

    Saved Widow Almost $400
    Saved Senior Citizen $4,091
    Saved Cedar Lake Woman $1,068
    Saved Client $1,068
    Saved Client $176.10
    Saved Client From $253.01 Lab Bill
    Saved Client From Big Medical Bills (totaling $1,017.46)
    Saved Client From Hospital And Collectors
    Saved Client From Pay Demand Letter
    Saved Couple $138.41
    Saved Crown Point Woman Over $300
    Saved Dyer Man $231
    Saved Gary Client Over $700
    Saved Gary Man $810
    Saved Hessville Woman $410
    Saved Hobart Man Over $1000
    Saved Kouts Woman Almost $400
    Saved Lowell Client Over $1,000
    Saved Lowell Woman $2,568
    Saved Merrillville Man $122
    Saved Merrillville Woman $510
    Saved Merrillville Woman Almost $300
    Saved Michigan City Man $815
    Saved Munster Woman $296.34
    Saved Woman From Error On Bill (of over $500)
    Saved Portage Man $93.19
    Saved Senior $267.31
    Saved Valpo Woman Over $1,000
    Saved Whiting Woman $66
    Saved Widow Over $1,100

You can read many of my Medicare problems articles for free at www.woodrowwilcox.com, www.medicareproblems.net, or www.americanclarion.com.

* * * * * * * *

SOME ARTICLES THAT WILL HELP YOU TO UNDERSTAND THE NEED

* * * * * * * *

SAVED WIDOW ALMOST $400

The widow of one of our recently deceased clients drove fifty miles one way to ask me to help with a bill that was not paid by her late husband's Medicare supplement insurance policy.

I reviewed the papers that she had and realized that the *Medicare Summary Notice (M.S.N.)* which pertained to the unpaid bill was absent. She assured me that she had brought all the papers that she had regarding the bills generated during her late husband's last few days alive.

Here is the problem that I pinpointed. *If the widow did not get the Medicare Summary Notice from Medicare, then it is very likely that the insurance company that issued a Medicare supplement policy to the widow's late husband did not get the Medicare Explanation of Benefits (EOB) form that it needed to pay the claim.* You can't blame an insurance company for not paying a bill that Medicare failed to send it.

The hospital was hounding the widow for payment of a balance of $392.45. The widow was worried. She was struggling financially after the death of her husband. She needed help and we helped her.

To solve this problem, I had the widow sign a letter to Medicare which I typed for her. The letter advised Medicare that she had not received a Medicare Summary Notice regarding the *Dates of Service* given on the hospital bill. The letter requested a duplicate copy of any M.S.N. forms for those dates.

The letter worked. Medicare sent the Medicare Summary Notice to the widow and the Medicare EOB to the insurance company. The insurance company promptly paid the bill once it received the information that it needed to legally pay the claim.

This service saved the widow almost $400 and a lot of stress. This insurance agency provides this kind of help to our senior citizen clients at no charge.

This sort of problem is common with Medicare. Many senior citizens throughout the country need this kind of help. When they don't get it, they end up paying bills that they really don't owe. That is one of the problems with Medicare.

In other articles, I have estimated that Medicare's shortcomings cost senior citizens over a billion dollars per year in *wrongful charges*. By "wrongful charges", I mean bills that would not come to seniors if Medicare worked well.

(Written in May 2009)

* * * * * * * *

CLIENT FELT BETTER AFTER VISIT

A senior citizen visited our office to ask for my help on a bill problem that worried her. The client was from Merrillville, Indiana.

I reviewed her papers and realized that she did not have a bill. She had an Explanation of Benefits from her insurance company. She bought a Medicare supplement policy through this insurance agency.

There was some language in the footnotes that concerned her and it concerned me when I read it. The woman did not bring the Medicare Summary Notice forms that related to the documents that she had brought. So, I decided to phone Medicare with the client.

In our phone call to Medicare, I requested that our client get duplicate Medicare Summary Notice statements mailed to her. When she gets those documents, she will bring them to our office so that I can compare them with the insurance company's Explanation of Benefits form and any bill that she received.

Then, I asked the Medicare representative a point blank question to get to the bottom of our client's problem in the fastest way possible.

"Will our client be charged for a knee brace that she got but returned because it did not suit her needs?" I asked.

"No," said the Medicare representative. "A medical device supplier and service provider must accept return of a device which is either substandard or does not meet the needs of the patient."

Our client had returned the knee brace but did not know that she should have been given a "Pick-up Slip" as explained by the Medicare representative. The "Pick-up Slip" allows the patient to get a replacement device without a new and separate charge on her Medicare coverage.

Our client returned to the medical device supplier to request the "Pick-up Slip". But, the firm never had heard of such a thing. In fact, the initial reaction was that once something is billed, it can't be returned. So, I explained to the representative what a Medicare customer service person had just told us the law was. I asked them to check on it for themselves. An hour later, the medical device supplier firm phoned me to say that it would give our client her "Pick-up Slip". That solved our client's problem. She told me that she felt much better after visiting our office and getting help with her problem. What is that good feeling worth to a senior citizen?

Our service to this client was provided free of charge. Does your insurance agency provide the same high level of service to its senior citizen clients? If not, why not?

(Written in September 2010)

* * * * * * * *

WIDOWER WORRIED BY $1100 BILL

On February 23, 2011, the son of a deceased client visited our office to get my help. His mother had died on November 30, 2010. The widower, his father, was worried about a bill from the hospital that had a balance of $1,100.

"I've tried to get this matter settled," the son complained. "I talked to the hospital and asked why they wouldn't work to fix the bill problem. They said that we had to contact whoever to get the bill problem fixed. Their job was to collect on the bill."

I copied the bill, researched our records to learn which insurance company was contracted with the deceased client, and contacted that insurance company to learn what it knew about the bill.

The insurance company reported that it never got the claim from Medicare. You can't blame an insurance company for not paying a bill that it never got from Medicare.

To help the family of our client, I typed a letter to the hospital to explain what had happened and requested that the hospital send certain essential information about the unpaid bill directly to the client's insurance company for processing. That should solve the problem.

If I had not worked to solve this problem, the widower would have been hounded by collectors to pay a bill for $1,100 which should have gone to the insurance company. How much is that peace of mind worth for the widower and his family?

My help to the family of the deceased was free and at no charge. The owners of this insurance agency care about the senior citizen clients whom we serve. We do our best to serve our clients well. Does your insurance agency give you or your senior citizen relatives and friends this high level of service? If not, why not?

(Written in February 2011)

COMMENTS

As you help senior citizens with Medicare related medical bill problems, you will realize that many problems are simply variations of other problems that you have worked to resolve in the past. But, sometimes, a rare or new problem arises. Don't be too proud to ask for help when you need it. I asked for help from my friend Gordon Bloyer when my efforts to help a client were stalled because of bureaucratic red tape. A client's life was at risk. Gordon Bloyer was more than happy to help me to help a client. With the new experience, I wrote the following story.

* * * * * * * *

VIDEO CLIP HELPS SAVE SENIOR CITIZEN

The internet, Senior Care Insurance Services, and Gordon Bloyer helped save a senior citizen from a life threatening problem with Medicare Part D – prescription drugs. It may be the first time ever that the internet was used to do that.

Gordon Bloyer used to have a public access and a leased access television show in Portage, Indiana. But, last year, Gordon Bloyer started using the internet. He became so well known that he was honored with a trip to Florida to participate in a Cable News Network (CNN) sponsored presidential candidate debate.

When our insurance office had a problem with Medicare and an insurance company that was life threatening for one of our clients, and no one at Medicare or the insurance company seemed to care, I asked Gordon Bloyer for help. Gordon Bloyer jumped at the chance to help and he didn't charge us anything. He was just as concerned for our client as we were.

You can watch our appeal at http://www.youtube.com/watch?v=XUs-O1Ilhl0. Also, the video clip can be found at www.gordonbloyershow.com and at www.youtube.com/woodrowwilcox. (YouTube® is a registered servicemark.)

Gordon shot the video at our office on the morning of Thursday, February 28, 2008. The video was posted late that Thursday afternoon. On the next Monday morning, our office got a phone call from a high ranking official at Medicare. Medicare officials became very cooperative to help us to get our client's Medicare medicine problem fixed. I believe that the video that Gordon Bloyer posted for us was the first time that the internet was used to fix a Medicare medicine problem and save a senior citizen from a life threatening situation.

(Written in March 2008)

COMMENTS

Some of the senior citizens whom I have helped agreed to let me video tape them talking about how I helped them or about Medicare medical bill problems generally. You can watch the videos at several websites and at www.youtube.com/woodrowwilcox.com.

I do not give you this information to boast. Rather, I want to help you to feel confident that this book is written by someone who has experience in these matters. Laws, rules, and regulations may change. But, learning the basics from someone who has done the work helps anyone to learn and accomplish more quickly.

CHAPTER THREE

LEARN THE "NUTS AND BOLTS" OF THE MEDICARE SYSTEM

To help senior citizens with Medicare related medical bill problems, you must be able to find the problem and select a way to fix the problem. To identify the problem, you need to know how the system should work so that you can spot the problem area.

In learning anything new, it is better to start with the simple and move to the more complex or detailed. Studying in a group is often better than studying alone. So, even if you read this alone, discuss it with others, too. You may choose to discuss it in a rather formal way such as a class setting or in an informal setting such as at a coffee shop. Discussing the material with others who are studying it will help you to learn it better and faster.

* * * * * * * *

HOW DOES THE MEDICARE SYSTEM WORK?

Here are some items that I wrote which give a good overview of the Medicare system to explain how it is supposed to work and what can go wrong.

* * * * * * * *

OUTLINE OF TALK BY WOODROW WILCOX AT KNIGHTS OF COLUMBUS (COUNCIL # 4047) IN MERRILLVILLE INDIANA

Presented November 25, 2008

1. Medicare is a human designed and managed system. Like all other such systems, it fails sometimes.

    a. Process: Medical service provider (doctor, hospital, lab, etc.) provides service and reports the service and proposed charges to Medicare. Medicare reviews and rules on the charges. Medicare pays what it owes (if anything). Medicare reports its ruling to the patient, the medical service provider, and the Medicare supplement insurance company so that the insurance company knows how to handle the charges reported.

    b. Much of the information is sent via electronic communication. Communication satellites usually are involved because the federal government and telephone companies rely on them for data transfer. If the satellite communication malfunctions, Medicare information can be jumbled or lost. Have you ever tried to watch a satellite TV channel during a thunderstorm? Bad weather and sunspots sometimes affect Medicare data communications.

2. Medicare does not pay for everything and not all medical service providers honor Medicare.

    a. Recently a client used a doctor who does not honor Medicare. So, the client got stuck with a big bill. Medicare won't pay anything and neither will his insurance company because the client's doctor does not accept Medicare.

    b. A Medicare supplement insurance policy *supplements* the coverage of Medicare. The policy will not pay anything until Medicare reviews and rules on the charges and reports the claim information to the insurance company.

3. Watch out for Advance Beneficiary Notices. If a medical service provider believes that Medicare probably will not pay for certain charges for services, someone at the office of the medical service provider may ask the patient to sign an Advance Beneficiary Notice *without explaining that it obligates the patient to pay whatever Medicare will not honor or pay.*

Recently, one client asked for help on a bill. When I checked, I learned that the client had signed an Advance Beneficiary Notice. So, I could not help the client/patient. The bill was a few hundred dollars.

4. Medicare and VA do not have a good communication system for sharing claims information. *This can result in a senior citizen veteran paying over one thousand dollars more than if the veteran never used VA medical services.* To avoid this problem, go to a private doctor or hospital in the first part of the calendar year to use up the annual Medicare deductibles. After the deductibles are met, the system works better.

COMMENTS

Please, note that the last paragraph (4) of the above article was written at a time when there was a serious problem with claim communication between Medicare and the VA clinic system.

I phoned many Veterans Administration medical clinic officials up the chain of command all the way to Washington, D.C. to complain about the problem for our clients and to learn what, if anything, was being done to correct the situation. One high ranking person at the VA in Washington invited me to tell veterans to contact her if they had problems such as I described. I wrote and published articles about the problems with the VA official's address and phone number. I sent copies of the articles to posts and headquarters of the American Legion and the Veterans of Foreign Wars. You can read the article at www.woodrowwilcox.com and some other places on the internet. It seems that the VA got the message. Now, very few senior citizen veterans tell me of claims communications problems between Medicare and the VA system.

* * * * * * * *

BEWARE OF DIFFERENT RULES FOR DIFFERENT PARTS OF MEDICARE

Beware of different rules for different parts of Medicare. There are four "parts" to Medicare:

1. Medicare Part A deals with inpatient hospital services.

2. Medicare Part B deals with visits to doctor's offices and similar services.

3. Medicare Part C deals with plans that combine Medicare Parts A, B, and D under one related insurance plan.

4. Medicare Part D deals with prescription drug coverage.

    If you are enrolled in a Medicare supplemental insurance plan that covers Medicare Part A and Part B, you can disenroll with one insurance company and enroll with a different company any time of year with reasonable notice. When you do this, make sure that the new insurance company has accepted your application and given you a new insurance contract before you write and send a cancellation letter to the old insurance company.
    But, Medicare Part C and Medicare Part D plans allow disenrollment and enrollment only during certain specified times of the year. Be sure that you know what those times of the year are. Be prepared to switch within the allowed time period if you do want to switch. Not switching during the allowed time will lock you into staying with your old insurance company for another year.
    So, if you have a Medicare Part C or a Medicare Part D plan, check with your insurance agent about when you can make a change. If you try to change such a policy outside the allowed time period, it will cost you time and money to fix. And, it might not get "fixed" in the way that you had hoped.

(Written in March 2007)

* * * * * * * *

MEDICARE MECHANICS

When a senior citizen goes to a doctor or hospital for service, and presents both a Medicare ID and a Medicare supplement insurance ID card, what happens after the medical service is rendered?

Office personnel of the medical service provider type information about services rendered to the senior citizen. The information is sent to Medicare for review and processing for payment. There are two divisions of the process because [the original] Medicare is divided into Part A and Part B.

Most insurance companies are able to receive the "Explanation Of Medicare Benefits" or "EOMB" or "Medicare EOB" for Medicare Part A and Part B services via electronic transmission.

Medicare and insurance companies use the senior citizen's Medicare ID number as a "Health Insurance Claim" or "HIC" number. The insurance company submits a senior citizen's Medicare ID number to Medicare (Part A and Part B) and identifies the person with that ID number as a policyholder with the Medicare supplement insurance company.

Because the Medicare ID number is used as the primary identification, make sure that your insurance company (and/or your insurance agent) has the correct number on file. Make sure that the office personnel at the office of your doctor, hospital, or other medical service provider have the correct number, too.

I have helped to fix problems where someone simply made a mistake about the Medicare ID number which caused the problems. One woman in Lake County (Indiana) asked for my help when she started getting claims and bills from a doctor in Florida whom she had not used. Someone at the Florida doctor's office miswrote the Medicare ID number of a patient. Because the Medicare ID number is the primary identification number, the small error caused some incorrect filings with Medicare and a Medicare supplement insurance company.

When a claim is filed with Medicare, Medicare processes it and sends the "Explanation Of Medicare Benefits" or "EOMB" to the insurance company and the medical service provider through the internet or by mail. This is often described as the "Medicare EOB" to distinguish it from an insurance company's "EOB". But, sometimes, the electronic transmission fails and the insurance company does not get notice of a bill. Medicare sends to the senior citizen a *Medicare Summary Notice* by mail. Somewhere on the first page of the Medicare Summary Notice, it reads

"THIS IS NOT A BILL – Keep this notice for your records". But, many senior citizens read the phrase, "This is not a bill" and ignore the rest of the message. They discard it when they should keep it for their records. If there is any problem with the bill, their insurance agent or insurance company can help the senior citizen to correct the problem if the senior citizen can provide the Medicare Summary Notice.

Many times, I have helped a senior citizen to correct a billing problem using the Medicare Summary Notice. In many cases, it was a simple matter of a bill not being paid by a Medicare supplement insurance company because the insurance company never got notice of the claim from Medicare. The electronic transmissions are accomplished by telephone lines and satellite feeds. A friend of mine who works at a satellite uplink station in southern California gave me a tour of the facility. In the middle of the night, trillions of bits of information are transmitted electronically to update the records of banks, credit companies, government offices, insurance companies, etc. It is quite reasonable that sometimes a malfunction will occur.

Sometimes, a senior citizen decides to switch from one insurance company to another for Medicare supplement insurance. When this happens, several bureaucracies in government and business must change their records. This takes time. Based on my experience, I believe that about half of the problems with Medicare and Medicare supplement insurance claim processing occur in the first 90 days of a person enrolling in Medicare or the first 90 days of switching to a different Medicare supplement insurance company. So, within those 90 day time periods, if a problem does occur, don't be upset. It is a normal occurrence which can be fixed easily with proper records.

(Written in September 2004)

* * * * * * * *

TECHNICAL MEDICARE MATTERS

Six months before an American citizen or resident alien reaches age 65, it is time to begin the process of enrolling in Medicare and selecting a Medicare supplement insurance company and plan.

Solving Medicare Problem$

A senior citizen reaching the age of 65 needs to complete two sets of paperwork to enroll in Medicare Part A and Medicare Part B. Medicare Part A deals with hospital related charges. Medicare Part B deals with medical office related charges.

When a person who has Medicare Part A and Medicare Part B gets medical services, the medical service provider gets the Medicare identification information of the patient and reports the medical services provided and the related charges to Medicare. Medicare reviews the information to determine whether the medical service was in fact medically necessary and what amount Medicare will approve for the charges. Then, Medicare pays 80% of the approved charges after the annual deductibles of Medicare Part A and Part B are met.

The other 20% of approved charges is the responsibility of the patient. But, if the patient has a Medicare supplement insurance policy, then the Medicare supplement insurance company will pay on the other 20% of the Medicare approved charges. Medicare must get and process the bill before the Medicare supplement insurance company will pay on the bill. The Medicare supplement insurance company relies on the judgment of the Medicare officer for a determination of medical necessity.

Exactly how much the Medicare supplement insurance company will pay on the bill is determined by the coverage of the policy that the senior citizen bought. The federal government has standardized the various Medicare supplement insurance *plans* so that there is less confusion to senior citizens about what is and what is not covered. So, a "Plan A" sold by one insurance company will cover exactly the same expenses that a "Plan A" from another insurance company will cover. This helps senior citizens and the people who care for them to really compare "apples to apples and oranges to oranges" when selecting a Medicare supplement insurance plan.

But, as I have warned in my previous columns, *Medicare does not cover everything*. If a senior citizen gets medical service that Medicare determines is not medically necessary, neither Medicare nor the Medicare supplement insurance company will pay anything on the medical service. A good example of this is plastic surgery to enhance a senior citizen's looks and ego. But, other things are not covered, too. A regular eye examination and service in selecting eyeglasses or service in obtaining a hearing aid are not covered. Prescription medicines were not covered by Medicare. Presently, that is in a state of transition. Officially, Medicare will not cover prescriptions until next year because of the new Medicare laws passed by Congress and signed by President Bush. There are now

Medicare approved prescription discount cards and Non-Medicare approved prescription discount cards. Check with your insurance company to determine which kind you or your senior citizen friend might have.

Before the change in the law, insurance companies created prescription discount cards and programs to help their clients to buy prescription drugs at a discount. These various prescription discount programs are in a state of transition as we move toward Medicare coverage of prescription medicines.

The various "Plans" for Medicare supplement insurance have different types of coverage for people of different lifestyles. Some people want in-home nurse coverage, and some people don't. Some people want other options and others don't.

(Written in February 2005)

* * * * * * * *

DON'T DISCARD MEDICARE SUMMARY NOTICE

The Medicare Summary Notice is one of the most important things that a senior citizen can get in the mail. But, because each Medicare Summary Notice has a statement in big letters which states that it is not a bill, many senior citizens discard this piece of mail and later regret it.

The Medicare Summary Notice is so important that your Medicare supplement insurance company must have the information on it to process a claim. Normally, after Medicare determines a patient's benefits and pays the Medicare portion, Medicare forwards a summary to the patient's designated Medicare supplement insurance company and a Medicare Summary Notice to the patient.

Medicare sends the summary to the Medicare supplement insurance company by electronic means. Sometimes, there is a problem with the connection or information in the electronic transfer of information to the insurance company. When that happens, there could be problems with the bill that relates to the patient's service.

The Medicare Summary Notice is a "back up" to the process of getting the Medicare supplement insurance company to pay its share. Also, it is a way of advising the senior citizen patient that either everything is fine or there is problem. Sometimes, the medical service provider makes a mistake. This could be a mistyped name or number that Medicare doesn't recognize, so the claim is refused. Sometimes, Medicare sends the claims information to the old insurance company and the claim is denied because it was sent to the wrong company.

The Medicare Summary Notice that is sent to the patient can help to straighten many billing problems. It is a tool that lets the patient get faster service in correcting any problems. Insurance agents and insurance company customer service personnel need a copy of the Medicare Summary Notice in order to help a client with a billing error.

If you, or a senior citizen that you are helping, can't find a Medicare Summary Notice that pertains to certain dates of service with a certain medical service provider, don't worry. Medicare keeps copies of Medicare Summary Notice forms for two and a half years. Getting Medicare to send a DUPLICATE MEDICARE SUMMARY NOTICE is free. Just phone Medicare and ask for it. Remember to have the date(s) of service and the name and address of the medical service provider (usually the doctor or hospital) so that the Medicare representative can assist you more easily.

(Written in August 2004)

* * * * * * * *

MEDICARE DOESN'T COVER EVERYTHING

Medicare does not cover everything. Be aware of that.

Recently, an elderly woman asked me to review a bill that she got from her doctor. It was for a balance over $250. Most of the bill was for tests that the doctor ordered.

But, Medicare did not approve the charges. Because Medicare did not approve the charges, the Medicare supplement insurance company would not pay on the charges either. So, at least for now, the senior citizen is "stuck" with the big bill.

Here are some insights to help all senior citizens who rely on Medicare:

1. Realize that Medicare does not pay for any and all medical procedures or services. Long ago, a system was established in which Medicare could review procedures and services. If the procedure or service seemed medically necessary, it would be approved. If it was not medically necessary, it would be disapproved. If it is approved, Medicare will pay on it after any annual deductible is met. If it is not approved, Medicare will not pay on it.
2. If Medicare will not approve and pay on a medical service or procedure, then the Medicare supplement insurance company will not pay on it either. This type of insurance is a supplemental insurance. The supplement insurance company relies on the judgment of the Medicare officials.
3. There are many, many procedures and services that Medicare will not pay for a Medicare client. For example, eye glasses are not covered by Medicare. Routine dental services and procedures are not covered by Medicare. For some procedures or services, Medicare will pay for only a limited number of times per year, depending on the exact treatment or service.
4. Medicare routinely refuses to pay when the doctor or other medical service provider does not write notes which clearly demonstrate the medical necessity of a service or procedure. So, if you have a problem like the one I discussed above here, first contact the medical service provider to ask that the notes be augmented to clearly show the medical necessity of the service or procedure, and then that the claim be resubmitted to Medicare. I have used this method to help many senior citizens reduce their bills.
5. Realize that the federal government can change the deductible as they did at the beginning of 2004. When that happens, realize that your Medicare supplement insurance company will not make up the difference. You will.
6. Have extra cash in reserve, or extra insurance, to help cover dental, eyeglasses, or other medical services that Medicare will not cover.
7. If money is a problem, tell the doctor or other medical service provider. Ask that they check whether the medical service or

procedure will be covered by Medicare. If it won't be covered, ask that an alternative procedure or service that Medicare will cover be used to achieve the same results. Ask that the notes given to Medicare make it clear that there is a medical necessity for the procedure or services. As long as Medicare will pay, your Medicare supplement insurance company will pay. That will reduce the chances of an expensive surprise for you.

(Written in December 2004)

COMMENTS

When I started helping senior citizens with Medicare related medical bill problems, there was just Medicare Part A (inpatient hospital claims) and Medicare Part B (doctor office, clinic, and laboratory claims). Now, there are Medicare Part D (prescription drugs) and Medicare Part C (a combination of parts A, B, and D which has a different claims process).

There are significant differences that should be noted. Medicare supplement (Part A and Part B) claims are filed by the medical service provider directly to Medicare. Medicare Part C claims are filed directly with the insurance company of the Part C policy. These are usually called "Medicare Advantage" policies. Medicare Part D has another system.

* * * * * * * *

DOCTOR'S OFFICE FILED CLAIM INCORRECTLY

One of the clients of this insurance agency asked me to help to resolve some unpaid medical bills. The case was a bit different from the usual cases that I handle. The client is a senior citizen from Hammond, Indiana.

In 2009, the client switched insurance coverage *from a Medicare replacement plan to a Medicare supplement insurance plan.*

There is a difference. In this case, the people at the doctor's office did not know the difference and made some mistakes which caused some medical claims not to be paid.

With a Medicare supplement insurance plan, the doctor, hospital, or laboratory files the claim with Medicare. Then, Medicare reviews the claim and sends the essential information to the medical service provider, the patient, and the patient's insurance company. Sending the claim information to the insurance company is called the *Medicare crossover*.

Most of the medical bill problem cases that I handle are caused by mistakes at Medicare in which either no information or incomplete information is sent to the insurance company. This is what causes problems with Medicare claims most of the time.

But, when a patient has a Medicare replacement plan, the doctor or hospital must file directly with the insurance company.

To help our client resolve the unpaid medical bill with his doctor's office, I wrote a letter to the doctor's office to explain this and provided the contact information for sending the claim to the insurance company so that the claim could be processed.

If I had not helped our client to resolve this problem, his doctor would have continued to bill him for a $145 unpaid balance. This insurance agency provides this level of service to our clients AT NO CHARGE. In this way, we demonstrate that we really do care about our senior citizen clients and that we do our best to provide good service to them. Does your insurance agent provide this level of service?

(Written in January 2010)

* * * * * * * *

A DISADVANTAGE TO MEDICARE ADVANTAGE POLICIES

A client visited our office bringing a bill for ambulance services which was not paid. The client is from Schererville, Indiana.

With the client present, I phoned both Medicare and the client's insurance company. I quickly learned why the bill was not getting paid. The claim was not filed properly.

The client had a *Medicare Advantage* policy with a good insurance company. Medicare Advantage is the name for *Medicare Part C* plans. A Medicare Part C plan is a combination of Medicare Part A, Medicare Part

B, and Medicare Part D which is serviced by a private insurance company rather than Medicare. Claims must be filed with a special office of the insurance company instead of being filed with Medicare as is the case with claims to Medicare and a Medicare supplement insurance company policy.

Quite understandably, the ambulance service provider filed the claim incorrectly because it was not aware of the distinction with the rather new Medicare Advantage plans. So, I wrote a letter to the ambulance service and gave the information that they would need to file the claim so that the insurance company could process and pay on the claim. Under Medicare Advantage plans, there is usually a co-pay which the policy holder must pay. But, because I helped the client to fix this problem, most of the $505 ambulance bill will be eliminated when the insurance company pays its share.

(Written in October 2010)

COMMENTS

Medicare Part D is the federal prescription drug program. Supposedly, it was designed to help senior citizens with the costs of prescription drugs. I don't believe that it really did that. When Medicare Part D started, many of our agency clients complained to me that their prescription medicines cost more under the Medicare Part D program.

Initially, Medicare Part D plans were supposed to be paid by Social Security deducting a monthly fee from a retired person's Social Security check. That seemed to overwhelm Social Security. Other methods of monthly payments such as bank drafts started to be used.

Even if the system did work well for paying for regular prescriptions that are used continuously, it does not work well when a senior citizen visits a hospital. In every hospital-medicine bill problem that I have handled, the hospital would not let the senior citizens bring their regular prescription medicines into the hospital to be used as part of treatment while at the hospital. And Medicare will not pay for prescription medicines in an emergency setting if the patient is well enough to take a pill from a nurse and pop it in the patient's mouth. Medicare's attitude is that if the patient is well enough to take the pill, then the patient is well enough to pay the bill for the pill.

Hospitals charge outrageous amounts for giving any such prescription medicines to patients. Medicare officials have told me that a patient can file for reimbursement or that the hospital can collect the medicine claim if it is enrolled in a Medicare Part D program for its patients. Really? A sick and elderly person has to complete some special, obscure paperwork to get reimbursed from their Medicare Part D plan for some medicines taken in the hospital setting? I don't think that is a workable solution. Also, so far, I have not found any hospital that helps its senior citizen patients with their medicine charges and their Medicare Part D plan in such a way. Medicare has even got special rules about when a person who is admitted to a hospital is not really an "inpatient" for Medicare Part A purposes. The Medicare system has fully embraced the "doublespeak" system of which George Orwell wrote in his classic book "1984".

CHAPTER FOUR
THREE TYPES OF PROBLEMS

There are three types of problems that senior citizens may experience with Medicare related medical bills.

* * * * * * * *

TYPE ONE: POLICY PROBLEMS

These are problems that are caused by laws, regulations, and rules that are made by some government office or official. You can't really help a senior citizen with one of these problems except by bringing the matter to the attention of government officials who should be told of the problem and asked to fix it. Also, you can bring the problem to the attention of the news media to build public awareness that there are problems with the Medicare system.

Other than that, don't worry about these problems because you probably can't help the senior citizen to solve the problem.

* * * * * * * *

TYPE TWO: HUMAN ERROR PROBLEMS

Everyone makes mistakes. You make mistakes. I make mistakes.

A worker in an office who is being pushed to do more because someone is sick and absent could make a mistake easily. An office worker who is distracted by a phone call or a question from another worker could make a mistake easily.

These problems usually can be solved easily once the problem is discovered and brought to the attention of an appropriate person at the place where the mistake was made.

* * * * * * * *

MEDICARE MISTAKE "KILLED" SENIOR

A "dead" client walked into my office. I have a copy of the letter of condolence from his Medicare supplement insurance company to the family of the "dead" client.

How can a "dead" man walk into my office to give me a copy of such a letter? The answer is simple. Medicare goofed again!

Someone at Medicare misunderstood that when a hospital uses the abbreviation "D.O.D.", it means "date of discharge", not "date of death".

So, Medicare advised the "dead" man's insurance company of his death. The insurance company sent a sympathy letter to the family of the "dead" man.

BUT, THE MAN IS NOT DEAD!

This story is humorous. It is sad, also. It makes the point that MEDICARE MAKES MISTAKES! When Medicare makes mistakes, it costs time, money, and effort to fix the problems.

If a national health care system which is modeled on Medicare is imposed on our nation, then millions more people will experience the problems which Medicare has caused for senior citizens for years.

(Written in September 2009)

* * * * * * * *

MISTAKES HAPPEN – GIVE PEOPLE A CHANCE TO CORRECT MISTAKES

A hospital billed a client for $912 that the client did not expect to pay. I asked the client to bring all the papers that pertained to the bill so that I could review it.

For minor billing problems or questions, calling the policy holder services department of the insurance company that issued a Medicare supplement insurance policy is the quickest and easiest way to resolve a problem for a senior citizen. But, sometimes, it is too complicated to talk on the phone and describe the various documents from a medical service provider, Medicare administrators, and the insurance company claims department. Sometimes, it is better to take the papers to your insurance agent's office to ask for a review. An experienced insurance agent or administrator can review the papers to find the most important parts and help to resolve the problem.

When I reviewed the client's papers, I discovered what I thought was an error on the part of either the hospital or the insurance company. I phoned the insurance company and learned that the bill had been paid. I got the check number and the date of issue. In a letter to the hospital, I explained all of this and cited the payment information. The bill was corrected.

When there is a problem, be reasonable. Everyone makes mistakes. When mistakes do happen, and it affects our clients' in a negative way, I try to collect the facts and then discuss the problem to a resolution. I do that because if I make a mistake, I want others to treat me in like manner.

(Written in April 2008)

NOTE THAT A MISTAKE IS NOT THE SAME AS A LIE.

THIS WORK INCLUDES HELPING TO PROTECT SENIOR CITIZENS FROM LIES.

* * * * * * * *

PROTECTING CLIENTS/PATIENTS FROM BILLING MISTAKES OR FRAUD

Joyce Brannon was murdered by her doctor. Joyce Brannon was a disabled person on Medicare. Joyce Brannon was going to testify to a federal grand jury in a Medicare fraud case against her doctor. On May 5, 2005, a federal trial jury convicted the doctor of murdering Joyce Brannon to keep her from testifying against him regarding Medicare fraud. In the same trial, the doctor was convicted of Medicare fraud and mail fraud (intentionally sending false bills through the mail).

According to the National Healthcare Anti-Fraud Association, health care fraud might be costing the insurance industry $100 million per day. Medicare fraud is part of the problem.

In 1986, Anthem Blue Cross Blue Shield established an anti-fraud unit to help find fraud, gather evidence, and cooperate with law enforcement officials. Anthem Blue Cross Blue Shield publicizes the numbers in mailings to its clients. In 2004, the Anthem Blue Cross Blue Shield healthcare fraud hotline got 1,344 calls from Indiana patients, 1,507 calls from Ohio patients, and 2,293 calls from Kentucky patients.

Carefully examining bills, crunching numbers, and using software to detect fraud are the usual tools of the insurance industry. But, in some cases, anti-fraud units of insurance companies are actually watching traffic at medical service providers' offices.

Although some doctors do participate in Medicare fraud, I believe that the vast majority are honest doctors who want to help people and make a decent living. The tragedy is that some honest doctors get hurt because one or more staff members who handle billing do something incorrectly. Most of the time, errors involve honest mistakes. But, sometimes the pattern of "mistakes" does not seem so honest.

When these billing "mistakes" catch the attention of insurance investigators or public officials, it could cost the doctor thousands of dollars and hundreds of hours to prove innocence. Even if no crime is charged, if mistakes were made, the doctor might have to pay restitution, interest, or civil penalties.

It is sad to me to think that incorrect billing practices by staff members might cost an honest doctor so much money, time, and trouble. When I see a bill with innocent errors or mathematical mistakes, I write a nice letter to ask that the problem be resolved.

I believe that it is in the best interests of both the patient and the doctor that the billing should be done correctly. An honest patient and an honest doctor have too much to lose when Medicare billing is not done correctly. Even an innocent doctor can be hurt financially. A patient might feel forced to pay a bill or get a negative item on a credit report when neither is justified. I am a friend to both honest patients and honest doctors.

(Written in May 2005)

* * * * * * * *

THE HOSPITAL LIED

The hospital lied. It lied in a letter to a client. In a letter demanding payment from a senior citizen client of this insurance agency, the hospital lied.

The lie in the letter stated, "Your insurance company has notified us that they have paid their portion of your claim. Payment of any remaining balance is your responsibility."

But, that was a lie. The insurance company did not notify the hospital of any such thing. The insurance company *never got the claim.*

Why would people at the hospital send such a lying and deceitful letter? The reason is simple: they want the money and they want it now. They don't want to bother with playing by the rules. Some will say or write anything to get more money faster even if it means that they don't follow the rules.

On behalf of our client, I wrote to the hospital about the false statement in the demand for payment letter. I told the hospital that our client's insurance company never got any claim from Medicare for the charges billed. Since the insurance company never got the claim, it could not have informed the hospital that it had paid its portion of the bill. I demanded that the hospital produce evidence to support the claim and forward that evidence to the insurance company.

Our client was covered by Medicare and a good Medicare supplemental insurance policy at the time. Our client should not have had to pay anything to the hospital for the services billed because of this coverage. But, some people at the hospital or at Medicare *did not do their jobs and "messed up" the paperwork.* Instead of working to fix that, the hospital personnel chose the quick, easy, and false way to handle the problem: they just billed the patient for an amount that was not owed by the patient.

If the client had not asked our agency to review the bill, our client probably would have paid the hospital a bill that she did not owe. Our service to this client was without charge. That is the kind of service that we give our clients. I hope that every other insurance agent and agency that helps senior citizens gives the same standard of service.

(Written in April 2008)

Note: My publishing of the above article caused several medical service providers to stop using the phrase which I exposed as a lie.

* * * * * * * *

TYPE THREE: TECHNOLOGY CAUSED PROBLEMS

The Medicare system is based on computers and communications.

A claim is filed by a *medical service provider*.

The claim might be filed by paper or electronically.

The claim is usually sent electronically.

For Medicare Part A and Part B claims, it is sent to Medicare. Medicare reviews the information and makes its ruling.

Medicare sends the claims information by paper or electronically to the *medical service provider*, the *patient*, and the patient's insurance company if the patient purchased a *Medicare supplement insurance policy*.

This system is now based on transmitting data through telephone lines, satellite uplinks and downlinks, and the internet system.

Did you ever use an internet connection and then lose the connection?

Did you ever watch a program on a satellite TV channel and lose a clear signal when a thunderstorm moved into your area?

Well, guess what! The same kinds of things can happen when one party in the Medicare system transmits information to another party in the Medicare system.

Did you ever hear that a computer can do as much work in one minute as it would take a thousand people a thousand years to do?

Well, a computer can lose as much work in one minute as it would take a thousand people a thousand years to lose.

When the data transmission from one point to another point is lost or interrupted, data is distorted or lost.

This is where most of the solvable Medicare medical bill problems originate. This is the area where most of my work to resolve Medicare related medical bill problems for our senior citizen clients is done. Basically, I reconnect the parties or put together the pieces of the puzzle. This is what I believe most people can learn to do if they really want to help senior citizens with Medicare medical bill problems.

CHAPTER FIVE

ARTICLES WITH A POINT

Before I explain the process of exactly what I do (and what I want you to learn to do), I want you to read some more articles. I have written over 300 articles about Medicare medical bill problems. Some of them relate to specific things that are no longer applicable. But, most of them are still pertinent.

I selected the following several articles for you to read because each of them discusses a matter or point which is important for your understanding of the Medicare system and problems that may arise.

* * * * * * * *

LEARN AND FOLLOW MEDICARE RULES TO SAVE MONEY

One of our clients sent a copy of a bill that was not paid by the Medicare supplemental insurance company. The client wanted to know why the insurance company did not pay the bill. I investigated the matter.

Unfortunately, I had to write a letter to the client to explain why Medicare and the insurance company refused to pay on the claim. The case is another example of why it is so important for senior citizens and those who help them to learn and follow the rules of Medicare.

People who learn and follow the rules of Medicare can save lots of money. People who do not learn and follow the rules of Medicare can lose lots of money. In which group do you want to be?

Below here is part of the letter that I sent to the client. Read and learn so that you can avoid the same mistake.

* * *

Recently, you sent a bill to our office for review. That bill is being returned to you with this letter.

The bill is for a balance of $99 for a routine physical examination. Medicare denied this charge. Under your insurance contract, the insurance company cannot pay on a claim that Medicare denied.

Medicare denied the charge because routine physical examinations are not covered by Medicare.

If this was not a routine physical examination, your physician should have written notes to indicate that the examination or tests were for diagnosis. Examinations and tests for diagnosis and treatment are generally payable by Medicare and the Medicare supplemental insurance. If this was not a routine examination, ask the doctor to augment the notes and resubmit the claim to Medicare for consideration of payment. If Medicare changes its position and pays on the claim, then your insurance company will honor that and pay on the claim according to the policy.

Because your doctor or clerk at the doctor's office advised Medicare that this was a routine physical, Medicare and the Medicare supplemental insurance will not pay on this bill. So, unless Medicare changes its position because of new information from your doctor, this bill is your bill and you should pay it.

To avoid this problem in the future, always ask your physician to be sure to write notes that indicate the medical necessity of an examination or other medical service.

(Written in September 2006)

* * * * * * * *

MAKE SURE OLD INSURANCE COMPANY GOT CANCELLATION LETTER

One of the clients of this insurance agency switched insurance companies to lower his Medicare supplement insurance policy monthly premiums from $134.45 to $99. But, he did not check to make sure that the old insurance company got the cancellation letter and cancelled the policy.

After a few months, the client realized that two insurance companies were getting a monthly premium from him for exactly the same policy from each insurance company. A senior citizen who has Medicare is supposed to have only one Medicare supplemental insurance policy.

The problem was given to me to fix. I am the senior medical bill case worker at a senior citizen oriented insurance agency in the Midwest. I was able to fix the problem. Here is how I did it.

I contacted both insurance companies, got the client's policy information from each company, and learned what each company's records showed about this matter. The old insurance company never got the letter of cancellation. Maybe it was lost in the mail. Maybe the client miswrote the address to the insurance company. Who knows what happened? I explained the problem to each insurance company and asked for possible solutions to end the double coverage. I had several possible solutions in mind, but I invited suggestions first.

The old insurance company's representative said that it would accept the new insurance company's new policy coverage overview page as proof to substantiate the client's intention to end the old policy when the new one began. Our client will get a refund for the months of premium that the old insurance company took money from the client's bank account while the new insurance policy was in place. Our client was delighted about the result and the refund.

This was a happy ending for our client. I was glad to be of service.

(Written in September 2008)

* * * * * * * *

AVOIDING INSURANCE PROBLEMS AFTER YOU QUIT WORKING WHILE ON MEDICARE

One of the clients of this firm came to me with a Medicare medical bill problem. I am in the process of helping him. I thought that sharing the basic problem and resolution would be helpful to some people who read this column.

The client enrolled in Medicare at age 65, but continued to work part time because of the excellent and inexpensive insurance that he got through his employer. Paying the small premium while he worked was cheaper than buying a Medicare supplement insurance policy. This made sense. This was smart thinking by the client.

But, eventually, the client quit the job and bought a Medicare supplemental insurance policy. The client experienced problems because Medicare never was notified that the client had quit the job and stopped having the employer subsidized insurance. So, when the client's medical bills didn't get processed correctly, the client had a problem.

To correct this problem, I worked with the client to get a letter of insurance termination from the employer's insurance company. Such a letter was not sent to either the client or Medicare when the client lost the employer provided insurance.

Once we get a copy of the termination letter to Medicare, we will have the client request a reprocessing of all claims since the date of termination of the previous insurance. The reprocessing will correct the matter and payments will be made for the client's medical bills.

While the client worked and had insurance, Medicare was the secondary insurance. After the client quit the job and lost the insurance, Medicare became the primary insurance. In each case, the claims are processed differently.

Other senior citizens who quit a job and change from an employer provided insurance to a Medicare supplemental policy can avoid this billing problem by being proactive. Ask the employer's insurance company to provide a *letter of termination of coverage*. Then, send a copy of that letter to Medicare promptly. That will minimize the chances of you having the same problem as our client in this case.

(Written in September 2007)

* * * * * * * *

WHEN SENIORS TRAVEL OUTSIDE THE U.S.A.

Foreign travel is important to many senior citizens whom this insurance agency serves. Northwest Indiana is next to Chicago and is part of the

"Chicagoland" area. Many immigrants from countries around the world settled in northwest Indiana.

I keep explaining to the senior citizens whom we serve that *the general rule is that Medicare does not pay for medical services outside the U.S.A. and its territories.*

A Medicare supplement insurance policy *supplements* the coverage of Medicare. With few exceptions, it pays only when Medicare approves a claim.

Since Medicare does not usually pay for a senior citizen's medical services obtained outside the U.S., it is important to obtain some insurance that covers foreign travel and foreign medical services before traveling.

One immigrant from China went to China and obtained medical services. Then, the immigrant returned from China and brought medical bills in Chinese to our office and expected us to help get Medicare and the Medicare supplement insurance company to pay the claims.

The system does not work that way. Also, I can't translate Chinese to English.

The general rule against Medicare paying for medical services in foreign lands applies to cruise ships, too. When you board a cruise ship that is registered to a foreign country and flies the flag of a foreign country, *you enter that foreign country.* Generally, medical services obtained on a cruise ship that is registered to a foreign country will not be honored or paid by Medicare or a Medicare supplement policy.

There are a few exceptions to this rule. One exception is that if the foreign ship is in U.S. territorial waters or is enroute between Alaska and another state when the medical services are provided, Medicare might cover the medical services.

To learn about all the rules and exceptions to Medicare coverage in foreign territory, ask Social Security to send to you the current versions of foreign travel portions of publications "Pub 100-02 Medicare Benefit Policy" and "Pub 100-04 Medicare Claims Processing".

(Written in July 2009)

* * * * * * * *

DELAYED FILING CAN CAUSE PROBLEMS

When a senior citizen who has Medicare and a Medicare supplemental insurance policy visits a hospital or a doctor's office, a lot can go wrong and sometimes does.

Fixing the messes that doctors, clinics, hospitals, laboratories, and Medicare create is a key function of my job. It is a full time job and then some.

Medical service providers have up to 15 months to submit a claim for payment. That means that the billing department of a medical service provider can "dilly-dally" for a year and almost three months before submitting a claim to Medicare. Many medical service providers submit the claim within three months. That is a much more reasonable and workable time period.

Recently, a medical office in Munster, Indiana submitted claims to Medicare ONE YEAR after the medical services were provided. In that one year period, the senior citizen had changed from one insurance company to another for her Medicare supplemental insurance policy to reduce her monthly premium payments.

Medicare got the claims over a year after the medical services were provided and mistakenly forwarded the claim information to the new insurance company instead of to the insurance company that the patient had at the time of services a year earlier. The new insurance company refused to pay on bills that were created before the client bought her policy with the new insurance company.

The client sent a copy of the unpaid bill to our office for our review. I caught the problem, reviewed the facts with both insurance companies, and wrote to the doctor's office to tell them what information to send to the old insurance company so that the claims could be processed and paid.

If you are a senior citizen who has a problem with a medical bill that has been unpaid by Medicare and/or your Medicare supplemental insurance company for more than three months, contact your insurance agent for assistance to check and correct whatever problem is preventing the processing and payment on the bill. The more you delay, the more difficult it will be to fix the problem. If you wait too long, you may pay dearly for procrastinating.

(Written in June 2008)

NOTIFY INSURANCE COMPANY OF CLIENT DEATH PROMPTLY

On December 9, 2010, the widow of a client phoned me for help. She was from Hobart, Indiana.

Her husband had passed away on October 23, 2010. She thought that Medicare would notify the deceased husband's Medicare supplement insurance company so that the policy would be canceled on the date of death. She made a mistake. Medicare does not act that fast to notify insurance companies of the death of a Medicare client.

So, in November and December, the widow's bank account was "hit" for insurance premium payment for her deceased husband's Medicare supplement insurance policy. Ouch!

These unexpected withdrawals caused the widow to "bounce" some checks.

After the widow phoned me, I went to work on the matter right away. I checked our records and contacted the insurance company that sold a Medicare supplement policy to the deceased husband. I informed the company of the death of the client and the date of death. I stopped any future drafts for premium and I got the insurance company to start calculating what it should pay to reimburse the widow. There is still some work left on this project, but I got the resolution started.

(Written in December 2010)

* * * * * * * *

DON'T BLAME INSURANCE AGENT OR COMPANY WHEN MEDICARE MAKES MISTAKES!

A client of this insurance agency called me for help with a billing problem. She was from Lowell, Indiana.

Solving Medicare Problem$

She had switched her Medicare supplement policy from one insurance company to another effective October 1, 2008. But, Medicare continued to send claims information to the old insurance company. Of course, the old insurance company was refusing to pay anything on any bill that was generated after the policy with our client was cancelled.

Our client phoned Medicare on November 25. After a long hold period, she was told that Medicare had no record of her switching from one insurance company to another and that her new insurance company should send a *claims crossover notice* to Medicare. After that call, our client called our office.

I checked with the client's new insurance company. The policy with that company became effective October 1, 2008. The new insurance company had sent a claims crossover notice to Medicare on September 19, 2008.

Then, the representative helping me told me that Medicare takes from two weeks to forty-five days to update records from crossover notices. But, our client spoke to a Medicare representative on November 25 which was more than two months after the new insurance company had sent the claims crossover notice to Medicare.

So, Medicare might claim that it takes two weeks to forty-five days to update its records on claims crossover notices, but it really can take much longer.

Really, it should take much less time because most of the time the necessary information is sent to Medicare electronically. Medicare does not need to retype everything.

Here is my point: Medicare is not well run and moves so slowly and badly that it creates problems for senior citizens. The failure to make the changes needed within a few days of receiving a claims crossover notice generates misdirection of bills and a tangled web of paid and unpaid bills between two insurance companies and the medical service providers who serve senior citizens on Medicare.

(Written in November 2008)

* * * * * * * *

ADVANTAGES OF USING A LOCAL INSURANCE AGENT

There are big advantages to using a local insurance agent.

Many people are tempted by television commercials or other advertising to call an insurance company to get a policy. Some of the people who answer the phones are not trained properly to answer questions accurately and clearly. Some people who answer the phones for those companies just learn enough and do enough to keep their job by keeping their boss happy. They are not really concerned with the customer and the customer's problems because it is not their customer or their business. Their reputation in their community is not at stake if they harm the customer.

A local insurance agent depends on a good reputation in the community. Even when honest mistakes are made (as will happen occasionally), the local insurance agent is motivated to do whatever is necessary to provide the best service possible for the client. Local insurance agents depend on their reputation among clients, friends, relatives, and neighbors to bring them new clients and build their business.

Here are some examples to illustrate what I mean.

Recently, two brothers in Hobart lost their mother and father. They tried to deal with the insurance companies by phone, but problems were not getting resolved. Their parents were our clients, but the brothers did not think to notify us of their parents' passing or to ask us for help. When they did contact us, we were able to help. We helped them get the problems resolved. We helped them without any charge to them. We helped them get money back from the insurance company that was *unearned premium*. We were able to help because we understood what the insurance companies needed in order to settle with the brothers.

A 67 year old woman from Crown Point visited us to ask for help. She had responded to advertising that encouraged her to try a new insurance program. The promises were so enticing. She agreed to get the information sent to her. The person who sent the information put the elderly woman on a new insurance program for a "trial period". After the "trial period", the elderly woman would be locked into the insurance program for almost a year. The elderly woman wrote two letters to the insurance company to tell them that she did not want their insurance plan. But, the company ignored the letters.

The matter was getting worse. The woman was being billed for two Medicare supplemental insurance policies from two different companies.

It was threatening to drain her bank account. Finally, the woman came to us – her local insurance agency.

With phone calls and letters, we helped the elderly woman straighten the matter. We spent time with her to help her with her problem. We helped her to keep the insurance policy that she wanted and get rid of the insurance policy that she did not want. The woman left our office much happier than she was when she entered.

It is not a perfect world. Mistakes will happen. But, when you have a problem with an insurance company, one of the best allies that you can have to help resolve the problem is a local insurance agent.

(Written in January 2007)

* * * * * * * *

HOW TO USE INSURANCE AGENCIES AND INSURANCE COMPANIES BETTER

Every day, I work with many people on insurance related problems.

I am surprised by the number of people that I meet who do not know the difference between an insurance agency and an insurance company. Also, many people do not know how to use insurance agencies and insurance companies better.

An insurance agent or agency sells insurance from an insurance company to a client. The insurance agents sell insurance to their relatives, friends, neighbors, and then to the relatives, friends, and neighbors of their clients.

There are two kinds of insurance agents. Independent insurance agents are licensed to sell for one or more companies, but the agent is not an employee of any insurance company. So, the agent can use independent judgment to help clients select an insurance policy with an insurance company. Other agents are actually employees of an insurance company. They get a base salary and commission from the insurance company that they represent. They are expected to sell that insurance company's policies. Some of these employee agents can sell insurance from other companies if the insurance company that employs them does not have the type of insurance desired by the client.

Insurance agents do not make any money by helping a client with a customer service problem. If they help with such a problem, it is because they want their clients to know that they care about their clients. They want a good reputation which will bring more clients to them.

But, many insurance agents never get training in customer service matters. Often, it is faster and more fair to the insurance agent to use the insurance company's customer service department. Some companies call this department the "policy holder services" department, or a similar name.

For senior citizens on Medicare, calling the insurance company about a problem is a rather simple matter. On every identification card for Medicare supplement insurance, there is identification information for the client and an address and phone number of the insurance company.

Most of the problems that might occur for a senior citizen with Medicare and a Medicare supplement insurance policy are simple ones. A quick phone call to the insurance company will take care of many problems. But, sometimes, a problem can't be solved easily. Some things are just difficult to explain over the phone to someone who can't read the same document that you might have. In those cases, call your insurance agent for help. Insurance agents have access to faxes and other ways to get the customer service department to understand the problem. Sometimes, agents can explain a problem more clearly to the customer service department at an insurance company.

This agency helps our clients in such matters without charge. We really care about our clients. I'm sure that other agents and agencies care about their clients, too. In complex problem matters, every good agent wants to help the client. But, for simple problem matters, I'm sure that every agent would appreciate a client for calling the customer service department of the insurance company first. If the problem can be solved with a simple phone call by the client directly to the insurance company, the insurance agent's time is saved for other business matters.

(Written in April 2006)

* * * * * * * *

SAVED MICHIGAN CITY MAN $815

The insurance agent who covers La Porte and Porter counties in Indiana for this insurance agency contacted me to help one of our clients who lives in Michigan City, Indiana.

The client is a senior citizen who has Medicare and used our agency to select and purchase a Medicare supplement insurance policy.

The client's problem was caused by Medicare. *Medicare did not send the essential claims information to the client's insurance company.* Medicare did this twice – once in October and once in November.

In each case, I wrote a letter to the medical service provider which explained that the reason the bills were not getting paid by the client's insurance company was because Medicare was not sending the claims information as it should have done. I requested that the medical service provider send the essential claims information directly to the insurance company so that the claims could be processed.

The two bills totaled $815. That is $815 that our client would have been hounded to pay by bill collectors if I had not helped him by writing the letters to correct the problem that was caused by Medicare.

(Written in December 2010)

* * * * * * * *

MEDICARE AS PRIMARY INSURER VERSUS MEDICARE AS SECONDARY INSURER

Over half of every day that I work is spent in fixing Medicare bill payment problems. There are many ways that Medicare does not work well when it comes to getting bills paid for the senior citizens who rely on Medicare.

One problem which keeps arising has an easy preventative solution that every senior citizen can proactively use.

When a senior citizen relies on a group health insurance plan as a primary insurer after reaching age 65 and enrolling in Medicare, the termination of the private group health insurance can cause billing problems.

The senior citizen could be covered by a group insurance plan through work or through the employment of a spouse who is part of a group plan that provides coverage for the Medicare enrollee.

Often, when the group coverage is terminated, Medicare is not notified. So, bills go to the wrong place and are not properly paid. According to Medicare's records, the senior citizen still has coverage from a private group health insurance plan. So, Medicare believes that Medicare is the secondary insurer.

When the senior citizen terminates the private insurance coverage, Medicare becomes the primary insurer. But, often Medicare does not get notified of this.

If you are enrolled in Medicare and your private group insurance coverage ends, get a *letter of termination* from the private insurer and send a copy of the letter to Medicare with a note that advises that from the termination date onward, Medicare is your primary insurer.

In the note, remind Medicare to reprocess any claims that have come to Medicare since the date of termination of the private group insurance coverage. There are big differences in the calculations and Medicare payments between Medicare as a secondary and Medicare as a primary insurer of a senior citizen.

Follow this advice, and you can avoid a lot of billing problems.

(Written in July 2008)

* * * * * * *

SWITCHING MEDICARE SUPPLEMENT POLICIES TAKES TIME

In the last few days, I noticed that several people who visited were a bit confused about Medicare, Medicare supplement insurance policies, insurance companies, insurance agents, and the amount of time needed to process applications, claims, and problem solving.

One woman thought that when she gave a check to an insurance agent on one day, she would be covered by the Medicare supplement insurance company the very next day. That might be the way it is in automobile insurance transactions, but that is not the way it is in Medicare supplement insurance matters.

A man who had helped his mother to purchase Medicare supplement insurance thought that when he gave a check to the agent on August 29, his mother's coverage would start on September 1, just two days later. Again, Medicare supplement insurance is different from property insurance policies. But, Medicare supplement insurance is similar to regular health insurance in the amount of time needed for any processing.

In dealing with Medicare or Medicare supplement insurance changes of any kind, one must remember that both a government bureaucracy and a business bureaucracy must change their records. That takes time. Medicare supplement insurance companies usually want thirty days notice to cancel or change a policy. Whenever someone switches from one Medicare supplement insurance company to another, the new company usually wants at least thirty days to review the application and accept the client.

Don't cancel a current Medicare supplement insurance policy without first being accepted by the new Medicare supplement insurance company. Make sure that you have coverage. Your insurance agent may ask you to write or sign a letter to request cancellation of the old policy, but that letter should not be sent until the new policy with the new company is approved.

Some people don't understand that the insurance agent has no control over whether an application is accepted and a policy issued. That determination is made by an insurance underwriter at the insurance company. The underwriter reviews the application, the medical history, and other factors to determine if the insurance company should issue an insurance policy.

The insurance underwriter relies on what is on the application. But, the insurance company wants to make sure that what is on the application is accurate. Most insurance companies have another employee telephone the applicant to ask some of the same questions that are on the application. The interviewer will check to make sure that the applicant's name is spelled correctly, that the address is correct, that the Medicare ID number is accurate, and that the medical history is accurate.

Sometimes, an applicant is rejected for a Medicare supplement insurance policy because the applicant gave a different answer on a question to the telephone interviewer versus the answer on an application. But, in my experience, I believe that usually this is caused by a misunderstanding or by a faulty memory. In such cases, some clarification can correct the matter and the applicant can be accepted for a policy.

Let me clarify this for you. Sometimes, if an applicant has trouble seeing or reading, an agent will ask the client a question as it is on the application. The agent will write the answer given. Later, during the telephone interview, the applicant might answer the same or similar question differently and cause the insurance company to wonder if the application was taken correctly and honestly. Because the applicant answered the same or almost the same question differently on two different occasions, the insurance company, often, will decide to protect itself by rejecting the application.

If this happens, contact your insurance agent. Sometimes, the different responses can be explained by clarification of the medical matter or history which is the subject of the question. Sometimes, the applicant did not correctly hear or understand the question over the telephone. Some senior citizens have an easier time hearing and understanding an agent who is with them rather than a person on the other side of a telephone conversation.

In any case, be honest about your answers. Being honest about the answers allows you not to need to remember what you said. Also, it protects you, too. Most insurance companies have a clause in their policy contract that states that the insurance company is relying on the honesty of the applicant's answers, but that if the answers are later discovered to be false, the insurance company does not have to honor the insurance contract and pay claims.

(Written in June 2003)

* * * * * * * *

MEDICARE UPDATE OVER SIX MONTHS BEHIND

An elderly lady phoned me with a problem on October 14, 2009. She is a client of this insurance agency. She is from Knox, Indiana.

In April of 2009, she notified her insurance company that she was canceling her Medicare supplement policy with it. She was switching to a different insurance company.

The "old" insurance company notified Medicare that it would not be our client's insurance company as of May 1, 2009. The "new" insurance company notified Medicare that it would be the client's insurance company as of May 1, 2009.

But, in the middle of October 2009, the client reported that Medicare had not yet made the switch. Her doctor's office phoned her and said that they were not getting paid within the normal time period.

The client phoned Medicare. A Medicare representative told her to contact her "old" insurance company to tell them not to send "cross-over" information to Medicare any more. But, the "old" insurance company stopped doing that over six months ago.

The client does not want her doctor or his assistants to be upset with her because of slow payment. But, the slow payment problem is not being caused by either the patient or her insurance companies. The slow payment problem is being caused by Medicare's failure to forward claim information to the correct insurance company in a timely manner.

This kind of problem happens all the time. Medicare is not a perfect system. No private or government health care insurance system is perfect. But, the private insurance companies seem to act quicker to correct mistakes than the government bureaucracy employees do.

(Written in October 2009)

COMMENT

In October and November of 2011, I helped a couple who had multiple problems. The couple was from Hammond, Indiana. The husband had retired and did not have health insurance for his wife or himself as of midnight on December 31, 2010. They bought Medicare supplement insurance policies that were effective on January 1, 2011. But, Medicare had not updated the wife's Medicare information to show Medicare as her primary insurer when the couple and I phoned Medicare from the insurance agency office on November 28, 2011. So, the woman's Medicare records were not updated by Medicare for almost a year. On November 30 of 2011, I helped another couple with several problems related to Medicare not updating their information. In the case of the woman, her health insurance through her husband's employer ended at midnight on

November 30, 2010. She had Medicare as her primary insurer and a Medicare supplement insurance policy as her secondary insurer since December 1, 2010. But, Medicare still thought that she had health insurance through her husband's employer. This skewed her claims. The records were not changed and updated with Medicare until I helped her to phone Medicare from our agency office on November 30, 2011. So, for whatever reasons, it took Medicare one year to update the woman's Medicare records so that her claims could be processed properly.

* * * * * * * *

SAVED RETIRED TEACHER HUNDREDS

A retired school teacher was getting medical bills and did not understand why. The woman retired from teaching in the public schools of Gary, Indiana. She now lives in Schererville, Indiana.

The client bought her Medicare supplement insurance policy through this agency. Her agent asked me to help her get the medical bill problem solved. I reviewed the paperwork with the client and phoned Medicare and the Gary Public Schools to pinpoint the problem.

Although the client retired in September 2010, Medicare never updated her records to show that she was retired. More than five months after she retired, Medicare records still showed her as still being covered by her former employer's group health insurance plan. That meant that Medicare was the secondary insurance instead of the primary insurance. That was "gumming up" her medical claims because Medicare was not paying as the primary insurer.

One bill had already been sent to a collection agency when the client came to our office for help. After I typed a letter for our client and sent it to Medicare, the records were corrected. Then, I typed a letter to each of the firms that sent medical bills that were not paid. In the letter to the medical service providers, we explained the mistake of Medicare which caused the problem and which was now fixed. This was not the fault of our senior citizen client – the retired teacher. We requested that each medical service provider re-file any unpaid claim now that the Medicare records were corrected.

As long as this is done, I am confident that the client's claims will be paid according to Medicare rules and her policy terms.

(Written in February 2011)

* * * * * * * *

CHESTERTON WOMAN FORGOT ABOUT ANNUAL DEDUCTIBLE

A client of this insurance agency sent a bill to me for review. She did not know why Medicare and her Medicare supplement insurance policy did not pay the entire bill. The client is an elderly woman from Chesterton, Indiana.

The client did not provide any *Medicare Summary Notice* forms that matched the dates of service for the claims with an unpaid balance. I contacted her insurance company to learn what information it had on the charges.

The client forgot about the annual Medicare deductibles. For Medicare Part B, the annual deductible for 2009 was $135 and the annual deductible for 2010 is $155. This means that the first $135 in 2009 and the first $155 in 2010 for Medicare approved Part B claims is the responsibility of the Medicare patient. Medicare will not pay any of this deductible.

But, the patient's Medicare supplement insurance policy may or may not pay the deductible. It depends on what policy the senior citizen purchased. All Medicare supplement insurance policies are standardized by law. This means that a *Standard Plan F* policy sold by one insurance company will pay exactly the same as a *Standard Plan F* policy sold by another insurance company.

In this case, however, the client bought a *Standard Plan E* Medicare supplement insurance policy *which does not pay anything on the annual deductible for Medicare Part B*. For that reason, the client was responsible for the unpaid bills because Medicare ruled that those unpaid bills were part of the annual Medicare Part B deductible amounts.

Policies that pay the annual deductibles cost more than Medicare supplement insurance policies that don't cover the annual deductibles. This is why a senior citizen should discuss the options with an insurance agent who is familiar with the different types of Medicare supplement insurance policies available.

(Written in October 2010)

* * * * * * * *

SAVED MERRILLVILLE WOMAN $510

An elderly woman received a bill from a local hospital for a balance of $510. She did not know why. Medicare and her Medicare supplement insurance policy paid for everything else on charges that totaled thousands of dollars. She came to our agency office for my help. She was a client from Merrillville, Indiana.

I reviewed the papers regarding the bill with her. Then, together we phoned her insurance company's claims department and Medicare to learn more about the unpaid claims. We were "on hold" for some time with each phone call.

My review of the paperwork made me realize that the insurance company believed that the charges were denied by Medicare. If Medicare does not approve a claim, no Medicare supplement insurance policy will pay on that claim. So, learning why Medicare denied the claims that totaled $510 was crucial to resolving the problem.

Medicare does deny claims for elective or cosmetic medical services. But, in this case, the charges related to a pelvic examination under anesthesia. That is hardly an elective procedure.

The phone call to Medicare revealed that Medicare denied the claims only technically. On each of the charges that totaled the $510, Medicare ruled that our client did not have to pay these charges because payment was included in another service received on the same day and which was paid by Medicare and/or the insurance company. Someone at the local hospital's billing office either ignored or overlooked this important information. The hospital was billing the client for an amount which it did not have a legal right to bill.

To help our client, I typed a letter for her to send to the hospital to direct attention to this important ruling from Medicare. If I had not helped this client, she would have been hounded by the hospital or collectors for

$510 that she did not owe. The false report of owing and not paying the $510 would have appeared on her credit report, too.

(Written in August 2010)

* * * * * * *

EXPENSIVE AMBULANCE RIDE

An elderly woman who is a client of this insurance agency visited our office to get help with an ambulance bill of $833 for a two mile ride. The client is from Dyer, Indiana. The ambulance ride cost $416.50 per mile. Medicare would not pay for any of it.

The woman lives only two miles from a local hospital. She had fallen in the early morning and called for an ambulance to take her to the hospital. Medicare did cover that ride to the hospital. But, Medicare would not pay for any charges for ambulance service for the woman to return to her home.

Medicare will only pay for trips to a hospital that relate to serious or life threatening issues for the patient. The ride home is not a Medicare allowed or approved charge.

I phoned the ambulance company with the client to discuss the bill. The ambulance company representative told us that the basic charge for a trip to the hospital is $1,000 plus $20 per mile and the basic charge for a non-emergency trip is $800 plus $16.50 per mile.

"How was I supposed to know that?" the elderly client asked.

To help our client, I inquired about a discount on the bill because our client is a senior citizen on fixed income and has medical problems which eat up much of the income that she has. The ambulance company asked for a letter with certain facts for a possible bill reduction.

I can't change Medicare rules. So, I helped the client in the best way that I could by helping her to negotiate a reduced bill.

If you get a ride to a hospital in an ambulance, get a friend or relative to give you a ride home. You can thank the person who drives you home by treating that person to a dinner at an expensive restaurant. Buying an expensive dinner at a restaurant probably will be cheaper than taking an ambulance home.

(Written in September 2010)

* * * * * * * *

CLIENT SIGNED AGREEMENT TO PAY MORE THAN MEDICARE APPROVED

A senior citizen client from Valparaiso caused a problem for herself by signing a document that she did not read. She agreed to pay $93 more than Medicare allowed.

The client signed a special document in which she agreed to pay for a medical service even if Medicare refused to approve it or pay on it. Because she signed the document, I cannot help her to reduce or eliminate this bill.

In past articles, I have warned readers to be careful of what they sign at hospitals, laboratories, doctor's offices, and other medical service providers. Often, a form is pushed toward the patient with the words, "And, we need you to sign this, too." Usually, there is no warning that the form obligates you to pay beyond the limits set by Medicare.

A Medicare supplement insurance policy will pay on a claim only if Medicare approves the charge. *If you sign any agreement to pay beyond what Medicare approves, your insurance company will not help you to pay for that charge.*

So, be careful of what you sign when you visit a hospital, laboratory, or doctor's office.

(Written in November 2009)

* * * * * * *

HOSPITAL AND MEDICARE DATA DID NOT MATCH

A client of this insurance agency sent a hospital bill with an unpaid balance to our office for our review. The senior citizen gentleman wanted to know why Medicare and his Medicare supplement insurance policy had not paid the entire bill. The man is from Lowell, Indiana.

I reviewed the bill and phoned the client's insurance company. Both the *date of service* and the *total charges* on the bill did not match with the information that Medicare sent to the claims department of the client's insurance company. The dates were off by three days and the total charges were off by over $100.

According to Medicare and the insurance company, our client owed nothing. According to the hospital bill, our client still owed money. Obviously, there was a medical billing problem.

I wrote to the hospital and requested that it contact the claims department of the insurance company to share information and resolve the problem.

All over America, senior citizens are getting hit with wrongful bills because of mistakes made in the Medicare system. Here is my warning to America. The federal Medicare system is not perfect. It has problems. If a national health care system is created which is modeled on Medicare, then everyone in America will have similar medical bill problems. I don't want that to happen.

(Written in February 2010)

* * * * * * * *

HOSPITAL DEMANDED OVER $2,000 AFTER BILL WAS ALREADY PAID

A client contacted her insurance agent about an unpaid bill from a hospital. The agent is associated with this agency and had the client send the papers to me at our main office. The client is an elderly woman who lives in Michigan City, Indiana.

On December 23, 2009, I reviewed the papers, made phone calls and wrote a letter to the hospital.

The hospital was billing the client for total original charges of $15,828.80. But, Medicare reported to the client's insurance company that the hospital bill totaled only $15,719.10. The difference is only $109.70. But, any difference between these figures can throw off all subsequent calculations. In this case, the hospital wanted over $2,000 more from our client. So, I wrote the hospital to alert it to the problem and request a review.

A Medicare supplement insurance policy will pay according to the figures that the insurance company gets from Medicare. If the hospital sent one figure, but Medicare sent a different figure about the bill to the insurance company, then there is a problem.

For some reason, the first letter did not get to the correct person at the hospital. So, a second letter was sent to the attention of a particular person. That worked. I was happy to write a letter to the client to explain what had happened and to report that the client did not owe the hospital a balance of $2,465.80 because the balance was now zero.

(Written in January 2010)

* * * * * * * *

BAD ADVICE FROM ADULT CHILDREN HARMED MOTHER

This is one of the saddest stories that I have written.

A senior citizen consulted an agent at this insurance agency. The agent helped her to obtain good insurance with a good company at a rate which she could afford. But, the insurance company was not a famous company and did not advertise on television (which is expensive).

This insurance agency is an independent insurance agency. The agency and/or the agents here contract with various insurance companies that want independent insurance agents to sell their insurance policies. So, the insurance companies must impress independent agents that they will treat the agents' clients well or independent insurance agents won't sell for those insurance companies.

Solving Medicare Problem$

We do our best to screen insurance companies so that our clients will be served well. When we get the impression that an insurance company fails to meet our standards, this agency stops representing that insurance company.

The owners, agents, and staff of this insurance agency care about the clients because the clients are our relatives, friends, neighbors, and people referred to this agency by our relatives, friends, neighbors, and clients. It is in the interests of this insurance agency to earn and keep a reputation for helping clients to get the best insurance possible under each client's circumstances.

That is what an agent with our firm did for one elderly lady. He learned about her health, her insurance needs, and what she could afford. Then, he matched her with a good insurance company that does not spend big bucks on advertising.

Unfortunately, the woman's adult children pressured her into canceling the insurance policy with the good insurance company that was recommended by our agent. The children pressured their mother into relying on Medicare only – without a Medicare supplement insurance policy to cover the other 20% of bills that Medicare does not cover.

But, canceling her insurance as of the start date and getting a refund caused the woman a major problem. After she cancelled the insurance policy, she was diagnosed with leukemia. Because she canceled the insurance policy that our agent recommended in order to get a refund, none of the bills she got were covered. Now, she has thousands of dollars of bills that won't be paid by any insurance company. Medicare will pay its 80% of covered charges, but the last 20% will be the elderly woman's responsibility.

Here is the point that I want to make. Adult children should look out for the interests of their parents. But, don't give uninformed advice to the parent. Participate in any meeting with advisors and learn with the parent what the options are. Don't dismiss the advice or effort of a professional in insurance or any other field. Don't pressure the parent to do something that is wrong for the parent.

(Written in June 2009)

CHAPTER SIX

WORKING THROUGH THE PROBLEM

In the best of circumstances, a senior citizen would get and save all the paperwork related to a Medicare medical bill problem and bring everything to me (or you or somebody) intact and in order.

LOTS OF LUCK TO GET THAT TO EVER HAPPEN!

WELCOME TO THE REAL WORLD!

Many times, senior citizens just mail a medical bill that they got and ask why Medicare and the Medicare supplement insurance didn't pay the bill.

Some of the possible reasons for the bill not getting paid include the following:

- Medicare did not approve the charge.
- The insurance company never got the claim.
- Medicare sent the claim to the previous rather than the current insurance company.
- A clerk mistyped the senior citizen's Medicare ID number on a claim form.
- The senior citizen bought a policy *that does not cover the annual deductible(s)*.

If you work at the agency where the senior citizen bought the Medicare supplement insurance policy, you probably have access to some other information such as which insurance company has the policy so that you can call to ask what information it has.

Insurance agents and insurance companies make special contracts with each other to protect the privacy of the clients/patients. For example, when I phone the Equitable Life and Casualty Insurance Company in Salt Lake City, I recite something like this:

"Hello! I'm Woodrow Wilcox. I work at Senior Care Insurance Services in Merrillville, Indiana. Fred Ulayyet is the chief agent that I serve. His agent number with your firm is XXXXX. Both Fred Ulayyet and I have signed non-disclosure agreements with your firm which you have on file. I want to discuss a matter related to policy number XXXXX. The policy holder is Bashful Client and his date of birth is 13/13/1913. (Yeah, the name and birthdate cited are fake.) The client is complaining about an unpaid balance on a bill with date of service 07/07/07 from a medical service provider in Munster with the name Megabucks Medical Group. Please, tell me if you got this claim from Medicare and anything else that might help me to discuss this matter with the client."

Got the idea? If you do this work, you need to be patient as you collect bits of information like the pieces of a puzzle to discern where the problem originates.

You can't make a phone call like this alone and by yourself to an insurance company to discuss a senior citizen's medical bill problem unless there is a contractual obligation for non-disclosure, a power of attorney, a limited power of attorney, or a similar document on file with the insurance company. So, don't even try it.

But, a senior citizen who has such a problem can call the insurance company to discuss the matter. That is the key to your entry into the arena to help the senior citizen. You can phone Medicare, an insurance company, a doctor, a hospital, or another medical service provider to discuss a senior citizen's medical bill problem if the senior citizen is with you during the phone call and gives permission to the other party to discuss that senior citizen's problem with you. When a senior citizen loses the capacity to understand, remember, and grant such permission, a power of attorney or other legal document is needed in order to allow Medicare or a medical service provider or insurance company to discuss the senior citizen's problem with you. But, until the senior citizen reaches that point of helplessness, you can help so long as the phone call is made with the senior citizen present and granting permission to the other party.

* * * * * * * *

SAVE THE PAPERWORK!

Saving paperwork might annoy some people that you know. But, if you must deal with insurance companies, Medicare personnel, and people who work at hospitals, laboratories, and doctor offices, saving the paperwork can be a blessing.

Recently, I helped a client who lives in Cedar Lake, Indiana, but spends the winters in Haines City, Florida, near Orlando.

While in Florida, he got sick and got medical treatment.

His insurance company had some questions about the claims and tried to write to all the medical service providers in Florida that the client used.

But, a clerical error at the insurance company caused a problem for our client. The bills were not getting paid. The client came to me for help.

It took some phone calls, some letters, and some time. I had to find the source of the problem. The client gave me some paperwork, but not everything that I wanted to make my job a bit easier.

Finally, I learned that the insurance company would not pay claims until their questions were answered and that a clerk at the insurance company had been sending the insurance company's questions to two doctors using the wrong addresses.

I solved the problem by getting the correct addresses for the doctors to the insurance company and alerting them that the delay was because of a clerical error at their firm. Such mistakes do happen. People get distracted or tired and make honest mistakes. So, I was not upset about the mistake. I was frustrated that it took so much of my time and effort to get things corrected so that our client's claims would be paid.

Just in case you need to ask someone for help in straightening a medical billing mess, save the paperwork!

(Written in August 2008)

COMMENT

In an ideal situation, the senior citizen would provide me with a medical bill, the Medicare Summary Notice form from the federal government, the Explanation of Benefits from the insurance company, and vital identification information such as name, address, date of birth, Medicare ID number, etc. The sensitive information is not to be disclosed to anyone outside the process.

For solving a Medicare medical bill problem, the three key parts of the puzzle are the medical bill with an unpaid balance, the Medicare Summary Notice, and the Explanation Of Benefits from the insurance company. The Medicare Summary Notice is the controlling instrument. You must learn to read and compare these items to find the problem or the source of the problem with a Medicare related medical bill.

The date of service, name and address of the medical service provider, the service provided, and the amount originally charged must match or there will be a problem.

To search for problems with paperwork, compare the information on the medical bill, the insurance company's Explanation of Benefits, and the Medicare Summary Notice form. It is easier to spot a problem if you triangulate the search with these three documents. If any information on the documents does not match exactly, that is an area where you should investigate more because there is a good chance that it is a problem area.

- Compare the date(s) of service.
- Compare the medical service provider names and addresses.
- Compare the doctors' names.
- Compare the total original charges billed.
- Compare the amounts that relate to Medicare approved, paid, discounted, and disallowed charges.
- Compare the footnotes on the Medicare Summary Notice with the footnotes on the insurance company Explanation of Benefits and any notes on the bill from the medical service provider.

For someone just starting this process, it would be good to have a clear desk or surface area to spread the papers and work with all the pieces of the puzzle that you have. I had a clean and clear desk once. That was when I first started doing this work. After you get some experience, you will be able to juggle the papers between the desk and your hands as you search for the problem areas and even talk on the phone at the same time. There are times when I wonder if the work that I do to help senior citizens with Medicare related medical bill problems would make an interesting reality television show.

Sometimes, a hospital bills the services of one department under one name and address and the services of another department under another name and address. Sometimes, doctors file a claim under their personal name but want the payment to be made in the name of a professional corporation. If a new clerk at a hospital or medical office does not understand the distinctions, mistakes can happen.

If phoning the insurance company reveals that Medicare must be contacted to resolve a problem, Medicare officials can discuss the matter only with the patient who is on Medicare or that person's legal representative (i.e., guardian, attorney, power of attorney holder, etc.) Medicare must receive the document and put it in the database before the non-patient person can discuss matters for the patient. That takes about ten to twenty days to accomplish after the appropriate document is faxed or mailed.

So, how can you help a senior citizen without getting a written legal document or getting into legal trouble?

The senior citizen can give verbal permission to the insurance company, medical service provider, or Medicare official. Medicare gives the senior citizen an option that the verbal permission is good for that call only, or for 14 days. This is so that a discussion can be continued if a follow up question must be asked. With some other requirements, permission for longer periods is available, also.

Your key to helping a senior citizen with a Medicare related medical bill problem is to have the senior citizen with you as you phone an insurance company, a doctor's office, a hospital, or Medicare.

At the time of this writing, the phone number for Medicare is 800-633-4227. Well, that's the one that I use. If it is different in your area or sometime in the future, find the current phone number and use it.

With a phone call to Medicare, once we get connected to a real person who works for Medicare, I start the conversation like this:

"Hello! My name is Woodrow Wilcox. I am an administrative person who works at the insurance agency where (name of client) bought a Medicare supplement insurance policy. I'll let you talk to (name of client) to get permission to talk to me about a Medicare medical bill problem."

I let the client give the identifying information and permission to talk to me to the Medicare representative. Then, I discuss the problem. Sometimes, the first representative that we get does not have the knowledge or authority to handle a problem. In that case, I ask to speak to a senior problem resolution officer. Sometimes, the first Medicare representative on such a call is rude or speaks with such a thick accent that neither the client nor I can understand the person. In that case, as politely as possible, I ask to speak to someone else.

Sometimes, a letter or fax must be sent after a phone call.

Realize that you have no legal right to send a letter or a fax with another person's sensitive health or identifier information. When such information must be included in a letter or fax, make sure that the senior citizen patient signs the letter or fax. They have a legal right to send such information and you don't.

When I write a letter to help resolve a problem, I use only common (not sensitive) information. The person's name and address can be found at various common sources. The date of service and the unpaid balance do not disclose any sensitive health or identifier information about the person and are often needed by others to find the "needle in a haystack". A senior citizen may visit a doctor, hospital, clinic, or other medical service numerous times and have a problem with only one part of a bill on one date.

Since you probably will need to send letters and/or faxes, the next chapter gives some examples for you to model.

CHAPTER SEVEN

EXAMPLE LETTERS

Here are some example letters for you to model and from which you can learn.

Remember that these example letters are designed to be sent to a senior citizen client or for a senior citizen client to sign and send to another party. I always give copies of such letters to the senior citizen clients. It is much easier for senior citizens to understand the importance of certain words and phrases if you capitalize those words and phrases. Typing words in italics may be fine to communicate with others, but I am serving senior citizen clients. To do that well, I deliberately capitalize certain things so that it is clear to even a senior citizen who has lost some eyesight that the word or phrase is important and that I am doing something to help that senior citizen. It helps to build on the relationship that our insurance agency has with the client. Strictly speaking, capitalizing like this may be considered "bad" English. But, it is good business public relations with senior citizen clients. I believe in the saying, "Form follows function".

Insurance companies, insurance agencies, hospitals, doctors, lawyers, and others enter into special contracts to protect certain information from falling into the wrong hands. Rules and regulations about who may write a letter, to whom a letter can be sent, and what can be in the letter will change from time to time. But, I believe that a patient will always be able to send a letter to protest wrongful charges on a bill and can include whatever information that seems necessary to contest a wrongful or erroneous charge.

For that reason, the following example letters are divided into two categories:

(1) letters from an insurance agency to a client/patient;

(2) letters from a patient to a third party.

The following letters are based on real letters that I have sent or typed for our clients. The names and addresses of people and parties have been changed to protect the privacy of everyone who was involved in the real letters. Any similarity in these fictitious names with the names of real parties or addresses is purely coincidental. I have no desire or intent to harm any person or party. Read the letters carefully to catch the hidden humor.

* * * * * * * *

LETTERS FROM AGENCY/AGENT TO CLIENT/PATIENT

* * * * * * * *

LETTER TO CLIENT TO ANSWER QUESTION ABOUT COVERAGE

Dear Mr. Senior Citizen,

You sent a bill from your pharmacy to us and asked if it was covered by Medicare Part D.

The answer is "no". This is not covered by Medicare Part D. Medicare Part D relates to prescription medications.

But, we believe that it is covered by Medicare Part B because it is equipment.

Ask your pharmacy or whoever provided the equipment to file a claim with Medicare. If Medicare pays on the charge, then your Medicare supplement policy will pay on it, too.

Thank you for allowing us to help you with your insurance needs.

* * * * * * * *

LETTER TO CLIENT ABOUT MISSING INFORMATION

Dear Client,

You sent some bills and papers to our office for our review. Unfortunately, not all the papers that pertain to the bills were sent. That makes it difficult to resolve the matters. It is like trying to put together a puzzle when some important pieces are missing.

Here is what you sent to us.

- Summary bill from Oily Gulf Coast Hospital dated 10/30/10.
- Bill from Really Oily Gulf Coast Radiology Assoc. dated 06/02/2010.
- Bill from Oily Gulf Coast Hospital dated 06/12/10.
- Bill from Oily Gulf Coast Hospital dated 11/30/10.
- Bill from Oily Shore ER Physicians dated 05/26/10.
- Letter from Oily Gulf Coast Hospital dated 06/21/10 which explains bill process.
- Two EOB forms from Oily Gulf Shore Life Insurance Company related only to dates 05/09/10 to 05/22/10 and 11/09/10. (Claims from other dates of service are not on these forms.)
- One Medicare Summary Notice which deals only with some claims of 05/22/10. (No claim from any other date of service is on this Medicare Summary Notice.)

According to the bills, you received inpatient services at Oily Gulf Coast Hospital from 04/27/10 through 05/21/10. The radiology bill gives dates of service starting at 04/23/10.

You sent no Medicare Summary Notice forms that cover any medical services on any dates other than 05/22/10. Many dates are missing.

Please, send or bring to our office all Medicare Summary Notice forms that pertain to any medical service received in 2010 during the months of April, May, and November. If you cannot find these, phone Medicare at 800-633-4227 and request DUPLICATE MEDICARE SUMMARY NOTICE forms for all dates in April, May, and November

2010. When you get them, bring or send them to me. I need all the pieces to see the complete puzzle.

* * * * * * * *

ANOTHER LETTER TO A CLIENT ABOUT NEED FOR MEDICARE SUMMARY NOTICE FORM

January 13, 2011

Mrs. Eve Applepicker
666 Deceived Drive
Garden City, NY 11530

Dear Mrs. Applepicker,

    You sent to me a bill from Saint Bernard Alpine Health Services for medical services on 05/17/10 with an unpaid balance of $197.
    I phoned your insurance company to check on this for you.
    Medicare disallowed the claim for services. Medicare claimed that the medical services that you received were not medically necessary. I don't know why because you did not send to me the MEDICARE SUMMARY NOTICE form that you should have received from Medicare. I need that form to review it to find any possible help for you on this bill.
    If you misplaced the MEDICARE SUMMARY NOTICE form that relates to this bill, please, phone Medicare and request that a DUPLICATE MEDICARE SUMMARY NOTICE form for every medical claim in May 2010 be sent to you. You can phone Medicare at 1-800-633-4227 to request that. When you get that, bring or send it to me at the Merrillville office.
    I tried to phone you about this, but I just got your answering machine recording and I left a message.
    Thank you for allowing us to help you with your insurance needs.

* * * * * * * *

LETTER TO CLIENT TO EXPLAIN ANNUAL DEDUCTIBLE

Ms. Madas Hellcat
5210 Honest Politician Avenue
East Chicago, IN 46312

Dear Ms. Hellcat,

    Your insurance agent gave me some paperwork that you sent and asked me to check on why a bill was not paid by Medicare and/or your Medicare supplement insurance company.

    I phoned your insurance company and learned that Medicare approved the medical service but counted it toward your annual Medicare Part B deductible. For 2010, the annual Medicare Part B deductible was $155. That means that the first $155 of Medicare approved Part B claims is the patient's responsibility. After the first $155 of Part B claims in 2010, then Medicare and your Medicare supplement insurance policy start to pay claims.

    All Medicare supplement insurance policies are standardized. You bought a STANDARD PLAN E from your insurance company. All STANDARD PLAN E policies pay the same no matter which insurance company you choose. All STANDARD PLAN E Medicare supplement policies DO NOT PAY THE MEDICARE PART B ANNUAL DEDUCTIBLE. There are policies that do cover the annual deductible, but those policies cost more.

    In this case, your doctor charged you $185 for services during your visit on 08/16/2010. Medicare approved the services, but reduced the allowed charges to $150.35. Medicare applied all of this amount to your Medicare Part B annual deductible of $155.

    This is the reason why Medicare and your Medicare supplement insurance policy did not pay on this bill. According to the federal Medicare claims review, the $150.35 bill is your responsibility. Please, don't be upset with your agent or our agency. We don't make the rules. We just help people to select policies that are best for them.

    Thank you for allowing us to help you with your insurance needs.

* * * * * * * *

LETTER TO CLIENT TO REDUCE WORRY

Ms. Soandso
123 Water Bucket Parkway
Longjohns, IN 46300

Dear Ms. Soandso,

 I got your bill for ambulance service from the Town of Longjohns and checked on it for you.
 It appears from the bill that the ambulance service filed the claim with Medicare and noted your policy with Mutual of Omaha.
 I checked with your insurance company. It has not yet received the claim from Medicare. Normally, it takes about six weeks from the time a claim is filed with Medicare to the time that Medicare forwards the claim to an insurance company for a Medicare supplement policy claim. So, please, allow time for this normal process.
 After six weeks, if you still have a problem, we will be glad to assist you. But, so far, there does not appear to be any problem.
 Thank you for allowing us to help you with your insurance needs.

* * * * * * * *

LETTER TO CLIENT ABOUT CHARGES DISALLOWED BY MEDICARE

January 18, 2011

Ms. Dorothy Todo
555 Ozzie Town Place
Chesterton, IN 46304

Dear Ms. Todo,

Medicare disallowed the $176.57 of charges on your recent bill from (the hospital).

I don't know why and neither does your insurance company.

To do anything else on this bill, I need to review your Medicare Summary Notice form(s) for dates of service 11/10/2010 through 11/12/2010.

If you can't find that, then phone Medicare at 1-800-633-4227 to request a DUPLICATE MEDICARE SUMMARY NOTICE form for every date of November 2010. When you get these documents, send or bring them to me so that I can review them with you in person or by phone.

Thank you for allowing us to help you with your insurance needs.

* * * * * * * *

LETTER TO CLIENT ABOUT HEARING AID

February 18, 2011

Mr. Vari Mistaken
7676 Confused Court
Dyer, IN 46311

Dear Mr. Mistaken,

You brought a copy of a claim to our Schererville office. The agent there forwarded the material to me at our Merrillville office.

I checked with the insurance company with which you have your Medicare supplement policy. The claim is for services rendered on 04/22/2010. The charges total $3,455.95 and relate to obtaining a hearing aid.

Your insurance company never got a claim from Medicare for this service. Medicare never got a claim from the hearing aid company that you used because the people at that firm already know that Medicare will not help to pay for a hearing aid.

There are medical services related to the ear that Medicare will approve, but the purchase of a hearing aid is not one of them.

If Medicare will not pay on a claim, neither will your Medicare supplement insurance policy. Your policy is a MEDICARE SUPPLEMENT insurance policy. That means that it SUPPLEMENTS payments on services approved by Medicare. If a medical service or medical device is not approved by Medicare, your supplemental insurance will not pay anything on the claim.

Not everything is covered by Medicare or Medicare supplement insurance. Other examples of this are the purchase of eyeglasses and cosmetic surgery.

So, I am sorry to report to you that the bill for the hearing aid is your bill.

* * * * * * * *

LETTER TO CLIENT ABOUT ANNUAL DEDUCTIBLES

February 17, 2011

Ms. Lora Tahdyne
789 Leota Lane
Griffith, IN 46319

Dear Ms. Tahdyne,

You brought a bill to our office for our review. The bill is from CASH4CARE with a balance of $162 for date of service 01/03/2011.

I phoned your insurance company to check on this matter for you. The insurance company reported that Medicare determined that the $162 was your 2011 annual Medicare Part B deductible. The Medicare Part B annual deductible for 2011 is $162. That means that the first $162 of Medicare approved Part B claims is your responsibility.

After you pay the first $162 of Medicare Part B approved claims, then Medicare and your Medicare supplement insurance company start to pay on other Medicare Part B approved claims throughout the remaining part of the year.

Standard Plan G Medicare supplement insurance policies do not pay the annual deductible on Medicare Part B claims no matter which insurance company you use to purchase such a policy. There are some standard plan Medicare supplement insurance policies that do cover the annual deductible, but those policies are more expensive.

When you discussed your options with your insurance agent, you may have emphasized keeping the monthly premium low. That would have caused the agent to suggest a policy that did not cover the annual deductible to help you keep the monthly premium low.

If you have any other questions, please contact your insurance agent.

Thank you for allowing us to help you with your insurance needs.

* * * * * * * *

LETTER TO CLIENT
RE: DISALLOWED X-RAY CHARGES

January 18, 2011

Ms. Helen Hurting
98765 Popcorn Place, Apt. ZZ
Valparaiso, IN 46383

Dear Ms. Hurting,

Your agent gave me a bill for $448 from [the hospital] which you gave to him and asked that we learn why the bill was not paid. The date of service was 08/20/2010.

I phoned your insurance company about this bill. Medicare sent to the insurance company a report that it disallowed (did not approve) $448 of charges for the DX X-Ray that you got with your mammography screening. Neither your insurance company nor I know why this was not approved. You should have received a MEDICARE SUMMARY NOTICE form from Medicare which should explain why. I need a copy of that form if you want me to help you further. If you cannot find that form, phone Medicare at 800-633-4227 and request a DUPLICATE MEDICARE SUMMARY NOTICE for all medical services received in August 2010.

When you get that, send or bring it to our Merrillville office so that I can review it with you. That will be the fastest way to find the problem.

Thank you for allowing us to help you with your insurance needs.

* * * * * * * *

LETTER TO CLIENT RE: $500 BILL

March 8, 2011

Mr. Watwent Wrong
1185 Clyde Court
Griffith, IN 46319

Dear Mr. Wrong,

Your agent sent to me a copy of your policy card and one page of a multi-page bill. Your agent asked me to investigate why there was a $539.89 balance on the bill.

No one sent me the entire bill. So, I don't even know by whom the bill was sent.

No one sent to me any portion of the Medicare Summary Notice that relates to the bill.

Despite that, I was able to learn something about the bill.

1. Your insurance company received the bill and an EXPLANATION OF BENEFITS from Medicare.
2. There were two original charges on the bill for 01/18/2011 – $500 and $100.
3. The $100 charge was approved by Medicare but the amount was reduced to $39.89. The $39.89 was applied to your annual deductible for approved Medicare Part B services. You have a Standard Plan G policy which does not cover the annual deductible set by Medicare rules and regulations. So, you should pay the $39.89 bill.
4. The $500 charge was not approved by Medicare. Medicare did not tell your insurance company why it disallowed the charge. The denial may be caused by a mistake, a lack of complete

information about the medical need for the service, or a new policy by Medicare. It seems strange to me that Medicare would refuse to approve and help you with a charge for removal of a benign lesion. In order for me to help you further, you need to furnish me with the complete Medicare Summary Notice that you got from Medicare. If you lost that, phone Medicare at 1-800-633-4227 and request a DUPLICATE MEDICARE SUMMARY NOTICE form for DATE OF SERVICE 01/18/2011. Then, bring it to me to review with you.

That is all that I can do for now. Thank you for allowing us to help you with your insurance needs.

* * * * * * *

FOLLOW UP LETTER AFTER CLIENT RESPONSE

March 11, 2011

Mr. Watwent Wrong
1185 Clyde Court
Griffith, IN 46319

Dear Mr. Wrong,

Thank you for visiting our office and delivering copies of the documents that I requested in my letter to you which was dated March 8, 2011.
Please, look carefully at the MEDICARE SUMMARY NOTICE with the review date of February 15, 2011 which is located at the top right of the form.
Note that for DATE OF SERVICE 01/18/11, the charge of $500 for extraction of a benign tumor has footnotes "a", "b", "c", and "d" to the right of the claim. Look on the following pages to the footnote section to find the meanings of these footnotes.

Two of the footnotes pertain to policies of Medicare. We cannot help you to change a policy of Medicare. That is beyond the scope of our assistance to our clients.

One of the footnotes states, "The information provided does not support the need for this service or item". That could be caused by a policy of Medicare not to help senior citizens with benign tumors or it could be caused by the doctor's office not including notes that support the medical need for the service in the filing of the claim with Medicare.

Another footnote states, "Our records show that you were informed in writing, before receiving the service, that Medicare would not pay. You are liable for this charge. If you do not agree with this statement, you may ask for a review." This usually means that you signed an ADVANCE BENEFICIARY NOTICE form (probably without realizing what you were signing) when a clerk at your doctor's office said something like, "Oh, and you need to sign this."

When a senior citizen signs such a form, there is nothing that I can do to help erase the bill. An attorney might be able to help you. But, we cannot.

I would suggest that you ask your doctor's office for a copy of the document that obligates you on the $500 bill. If they cannot produce the document for you, then you might get lucky and get the bill reduced or eliminated.

Thank you for allowing us to help you with your insurance needs.

* * * * * * * *

LETTER ABOUT MSN PAGE ONE MISSING

Miss Kari Okee
208 Custer Hill
Muskogee, OK 74402

Dear Miss Okee,

Papers were given to me about a bill for $361 for medical services to you. I was asked to check on it.

The papers were incomplete. Page 1 of the Medicare Summary Notice was missing. I got Page 2 and Page 3, but not Page 1. The insurance company's Explanation of Benefits states that a $361 charge is not covered by the insurance policy because it was not approved by Medicare. Without Page 1 of the Medicare Summary Notice form that you received from the federal government, I have no idea why Medicare did not approve the medical service that relates to a $361 charge.

Please, send to me Page 1 of the Medicare Summary Notice form that was processed on August 16, 2011 (upper right corner of each page) and which relates to the date of service 5/28/11.

If you have lost that page, phone Medicare and ask for a DUPLICATE MEDICARE SUMMARY NOTICE FORM THAT HAS THE CLAIM FOR 5/28/11. When you get it, send or bring it to me.

Thank you for allowing us to help you with your insurance needs.

* * * * * * * *

LETTER TO CLIENT REGARDING EYE CLINIC BILL

December 23, 2011

Ms. Condoleezza Castelli
11577 Jayworth Drive
Indianapolis, IN 46205

Dear Ms. Castelli,

You sent to us a bill from an eye clinic and told us that your daughter already paid the bill. You asked us to get your daughter reimbursed. That's not really how Medicare supplement insurance policies work. But, we will try to help you.

We got the bill with your note on December 21, 2011. Both the date of service and the statement date on the bill are December 16, 2011. That's just five days after the medical services were rendered at the eye clinic. The Medicare system does not work that fast.

First, please phone the eye clinic and ask them if they have filed the claim with Medicare. If they did not yet file the claim with Medicare, neither Medicare nor your Medicare supplement insurance policy will pay anything on the bill. The eye clinic must file the claim with Medicare! Your daughter's payment of the bill may have caused the eye clinic to not bother with filing the claim with Medicare. So, that is the first problem to be overcome.

Second, based on my experience, the usual amount of time for the cycle of a claim being filed with Medicare to the insurance company getting the claim from Medicare and paying on the claim is about six weeks. That seems to be the average. It can be longer or shorter. But, it is never just five days.

Please, contact the eye clinic to make sure that they file the claim with Medicare and then allow enough time for the normal process.

Thank you for allowing us to help you with your insurance needs.

* * * * * * * *

LETTER TO CLIENT – NEED OLD BILL INFO

December 23, 2011

Mrs. Wilhelmia Velkommenzy
1928 Baker Park Blvd.
Cicero, IN 46034

Dear Mrs. Velkommenzy,

You sent a bill to me for my review. But, you did not send complete information.

On the bill that you sent to me, there is a previous balance for services of $107.68. I have no idea what dates or services relate to this unpaid balance.

To resolve this part of the bill, please contact your doctor's office to get copies of all bills that have an unpaid balance that is part or all of the $107.68. The information will provide the dates of service which will allow me to start checking on the matter.

On the bill that you sent to me, there is an unpaid balance on current charges of only $26.96. I was not able to reach your insurance company right before Christmas. I will inquire on this part of the bill after Christmas.

In the future, please send both the bill and the Medicare Summary Notice from Medicare which relates to any bill in question.

Thank you for allowing us to help you with your insurance needs.

* * * * * * * *

LETTER TO GIVE CLIENT GOOD NEWS

December 29, 2011

Ms. Sallie Olivia Singer
44 Country Music Lover Lane
Franklin, TN 37067

Dear Ms. Singer,

Our letter to the hospital got a response. I got a phone call. I got additional information about the claim and phoned your insurance company. After I spoke to the insurance company, I was assured that the $1,132 claim will be paid within 20 days.

Also, I got assurance that a letter of apology and explanation will be sent to you which would be appropriate for you to send to any credit bureau to help you to remove any "ding" for this bill going to a collection agency. But, I got assurance from the hospital that as long as the bill is paid in that 20 day period, the hospital will recall the bill from the outside collection agency and no "ding" will be put on your credit report.

In my phone calls with the insurance company and the hospital, I discovered several errors on their parts.

- The bill to you which you gave to me had only the date of service July 8, 2011. But, the information that was sent to Medicare and the insurance company had dates of service July 3 through 8, 2011. So, when I phoned the insurance company to ask if they got your bill for date of service July 8, 2011, their representatives

could not find it. The hospital said that the wrong date on the bill to you may have been caused by one of their outside service contractors.
- The insurance company's first reviewer of the bill mistakenly classified it as outside the insurance policy's coverage period. That was the insurance company's mistake and they apologized and took responsibility for that mistake by one of their employees.

I believe that finishes this problem case. Please, tell your friends and relatives that this agency went the extra distance to give you good service to resolve this medical bill problem that could have cost you $1,132 if nothing were done to fix it. The Medicare system is run by humans and it is not perfect. When mistakes happen, we do our best to protect our clients from financial harm that could come to them from those mistakes.

Thank you for allowing us to help you with your insurance needs.

* * * * * * * *

LETTER TO CLIENT RE: MISSING PAGE OF MSN AND LETTERS

January 10, 2011

Miss Elae Neeyus
4321 Percival Place
Westville, IN 46391

Dear Miss Elae Neeyus,

Your agent with our firm delivered to me some papers that pertained to some unpaid medical bills that were sent to you.

One very important item was missing from the papers. Page 3 (Page 3 of 4) of the Medicare Summary Notice form dated November 16, 2010 was missing. That page has the footnotes section which explains the footnotes that Medicare reviewers made next to the claim summaries. I need that page. Please, make a copy and send it to me at our Merrillville office.

I still worked on the two bills.

Here is a brief summary of what I learned when I phoned your insurance company.

- Medicare disallowed the charges on the bill from Dr. XXXX of XXXX hospital system. I don't know why because I never got the third page of the Medicare Summary Notice that has the footnotes.
- The XXXX medical service sent a bill that covered three dates of service. For 09/13/10, your insurance company paid the balances of $16.53 and $15.85. For 10/19/10, Medicare sent to your insurance company only $442 of the $612 in charges on the bill from XXXX medical service. For 11/08/10, Medicare never sent the claim to your insurance company.

Please, remember that this agency and your insurance company did not cause these problems. But, we are working to help you to get things corrected. Please, make things easier by sending a copy of the third page of the Medicare Summary Notice.

After I get the missing page from the M.S.N. form, I can prepare letters for your signature to send to the medical service providers to help resolve the bill problems.

Thank you for allowing us to help you with your insurance needs.

* * * * * * * *

LETTERS FROM CLIENT/PATIENT TO THIRD PARTIES

* * * * * * * *

LETTER TO MEDICAL SERVICE PROVIDER

December 23, 2010

Patient Accounts
Megabucks Medical Services
P. O. Box XXX
Merrillville, IN 46411

Dear Representative,

I went to my insurance agent's office for help to understand why your bill to me was not paid. They helped me.

The bill is for DATE OF SERVICE 04/29/2010 with an unpaid balance of $12.42.

They checked with my insurance company. MEDICARE NEVER SENT THIS CLAIM TO THE INSURANCE COMPANY.

To fix this problem that was caused by MEDICARE, please, send both the original billing information and the Medicare EOB information that you have for this claim DIRECTLY TO MY INSURANCE COMPANY. Here is the contact information that you need to do that.

>   Claims Dept.
>   Woody Cares Ins. Co.
>   P. O. Box XXXX
>   Woody, CA 93287

Please, do not "ding" my credit history. It is not my fault that MEDICARE did not send the claim to the insurance company so that the claim could be processed. Thank you for your cooperation in this matter.

>   Sincerely,
>
>   Nomo Monee
>   P. O. Box XXXX
>   Merrillville, IN 46411

* * * * * * * *

LETTER FOR CLIENT TO SIGN FOR FIXING MEDICARE PART D PROBLEM

January 11, 2011

Medicare Part D Insurance Company A
P. O. Box XXXX
Woodland, CA 95695

And

Medicare Part D Insurance Company B
P. O. Box XXXX
Zephyr Cove, NV 89448

Re: Keeping policy with Medicare Part D Insurance Company A and terminating policy with Medicare Part D Insurance Company B.

Dear Representatives,

    On or about November 24, 2010, I applied for a Medicare Part D plan with Medicare Part D Insurance Company A at my insurance agent's office.
    On or about December 18, I wanted to know if my application was processed. But, I could not remember the name of the insurance company. For some reason, I thought that my insurance agent helped me to apply for a Medicare Part D plan with Medicare Part D Insurance Company B. So, I phoned Company B. I did not know that the Company B representative was enrolling me with Company B over the phone. When I realized this, I phoned Company B on December 23 to cancel that application. I was given the cancellation confirmation reference number XXX-XXX-XXX-XXX by the Company B representative on that date.
    But, Company B keeps sending me mail as though I still have a Part D plan with it.
    Then, on the same day in early January, I received both a welcoming letter and a cancellation letter from Company A for Medicare Part D policy number XXXXXX-XX.

Woodrow Wilcox, a staff member at my agent's office, helped me to phone Medicare about this. According to the Medicare representative, neither insurance company lists me as having a policy. So, I have no Medicare Part D coverage at all. I have only seven days of medicine left. So, I complained to Medicare about this.

Accompanying this letter are the first pages of letters that I received from your offices to help you to use the information on the pages as references to help you expedite this matter. Please, do something to fix this problem right away. I need medicine and I want the Medicare Part D Insurance Company A plan that Senior Care Insurance Services in Merrillville helped me to apply to get. Thank you for your cooperation.

                                Sincerely,

                                Sweet And Forgetful

                                425 Whutzittuya Lane
                                Crown Point, IN 46307

                        * * * * * * * *

LETTER TO MEDICAL SERVICE PROVIDER RE: TWO INSURANCE COMPANIES AND CLAIMS

Patient Accounts
Healthy Profits Health Care, P.C.
1234 Payusnowor Court
Merrillville, IN 46410

Dear Representative,

I brought a bill from your office to my insurance agent's office and asked for a review. The bill is for DATES OF SERVICE 07/04/2010, 08/09/2010, and 09/17/2010 with unpaid balances totaling $824.

My insurance agency checked with my insurance companies. On 09/01/2010, I switched insurance companies for my Medicare supplement insurance.

Medicare did not send the claims with the unpaid balance to either of the insurance companies. The insurance companies can't be expected to pay claims that they never received from Medicare. This is not my fault; nor is it your fault.

To fix this mistake that was caused by Medicare in the fastest way possible so that the claims can be processed, please send both the ORIGINAL BILLING INFORMATION and the MEDICARE EOB INFORMATION that you have regarding these claims DIRECTLY TO THE RESPECTIVE INSURANCE COMPANIES.

For dates of service prior to 09/01/2010, send the information to:

        Claims Dept.
        Wannapayit Ins. Co.
        P.O. Box XXX
        White House, Tennessee 37188

For dates of service on or after 09/01/2010, send the information to:

        Claims Dept.
        Wegotdadough Ins. Co.
        P. O. Box XXX
        Bakers Corner, Indiana 46069

Thank you for your cooperation in this matter.

        Sincerely,

        Firr Getful
        444 N. Delores Drive
        Griffith, IN 46319

        * * * * * * * *

LETTER TO MEDICAL SERVICE PROVIDER WHEN INFORMATION ABSENT

Patient Accounts
Magical Medical Complex, P.C.
12345 Makinmoney Parkway
Orlando, FL 32808

Dear Representative,

    I took your bill to me to my insurance agent's office and asked them to review it. The DATE OF SERVICE is 06/16/10 with an unpaid balance of $84.

    They checked with my insurance company. It reported that Medicare approved all other charges for this date from your firm except the $84 charge. The agency administrator did not review the original bill with a Medicare Summary Notice with me because I did not have one and I don't remember getting one.

    So, I am requesting that you review the charges. Please, check to see if the $84 charge is something that Medicare might approve if the notes with the claim are augmented to more precisely demonstrate the medical necessity of the medical service.

    Thank you for your assistance in this matter.

                                     Sincerely,

                                       Sick O. Bills
                                       86 Hardluck Way
                                       Wanatah, IN 46390

                    * * * * * * * *

LETTER TO MEDICAL CLINIC
RE: THREE BALANCES

Patient Accounts
Medicine Man Medical Service
1234 Drums and Dances Drive
Dyer, IN 46311

Dear Representative,

    I took a bill from your firm to my insurance agent's office for a review. I wanted to know why Medicare and my Medicare supplement insurance did not pay this bill.
    With the help of my insurance agent's administrator, I reviewed the bill and phoned my insurance company for more information. There are three dates of service on the bill. Here is what we learned.

- For 09/13/10, the insurance company paid the balances of $16.53 and $15.85 with electronic check number XXXXXXXX earlier this month (January 2011).
- For 10/19/10, Medicare sent to the insurance company only $442 of the $612 in charges that are on the bill that you sent to me.
- For 11/08/10, Medicare never sent the claim to the insurance company.

    To fix these errors that were caused by Medicare, please, send both the original billing information and the Medicare EOB information that you have on any unpaid claims DIRECTLY TO MY INSURANCE COMPANY. Here is the contact information.

                              Claims Dept.
                              Ohio River Paddlewheel Ins. Co.
                              P.O. Box XXX
                              Louisville, KY 402XX

Thank you for your cooperation.

                                            Sincerely,

Claire Voyant
5432 South Griffith Blvd.
Griffith, IN 46319

* * * * * * * *

LETTER ABOUT TWO PROBLEMS WITH BILL

February 18, 2011

Patient Accounts
Cure For Cash Clinic
1909 Marjorie Manor
Hebron, IN 46341

Dear Representative,

    I took a bill that I got from your office to my insurance agent's office for a review. The date of service is 09/30/2010 with an unpaid balance of $131.23.
    Together, we reviewed the bill and the Medicare Summary Notice form that relates to the bill. Then, we consulted the Medicare supplement company that has my policy. We discovered two problems.

1. A footnote on the Medicare Summary Notice regarding a charge of $90.69 states, "Medicare cannot pay for this service for the diagnosis shown on the claim." Please, review your notes regarding this medical service. Please, augment the notes to demonstrate the medical need for this service or otherwise clarify the matter so that the notes with the claim for the service conform to Medicare standards to allow approval.

2. Medicare never sent the claim to the insurance company. The insurance company never received a claim from Medicare for services from your firm to me on this date of service. To correct this mistake of Medicare in the quickest way possible, please, after you have augmented the notes on the bill, or

otherwise fixed the problem noted in the above paragraph, send both the original billing information and the Medicare EOB information that you have on this claim directly to my insurance company. Here is the contact information.

    Claims Dept.
    Wecountdemonet Ins. Co.
    P. O. Box XXXX
    New Orleans, Louisiana 70112

Thank you for your cooperation in this matter.

    Sincerely,

    Deborah D. Zeeezed
    69 Passion Place
    Roselawn, IN 46372

   * * * * * * * *

LETTER TO MEDICAL OFFICE TO HELP CLIENT WITH BILL PROBLEM

            February 17, 2011

Patient Accounts
Dr. Marie Moneylover, P.C.
11 Dracula Drive
Michigan City, IN 46360

Dear Representative,

 I sent to my insurance agent's office some bills from your office with unpaid balances and asked them to review the bills. There are various dates of service on the bills.
 The administrator at my insurance agent's office believes that he found the problem and can suggest a solution.

The bills from your office have one date of service prior to October 1, 2010 and all other dates of service are after October 1, 2010. It seems that the bills for services after October 1, 2010 are not getting paid. That makes the administrator believe that the problem is with the Medicare crossover of claims. If that is so, then the problem can be fixed rather easily. Please, remember that I did not cause this problem. Neither did your firm cause the problem. But, you can help to correct this.

On October 1, 2010, I switched Medicare supplement policies from one insurance company to another. If Medicare continued to send claims to the old insurance company for claims with dates of service after October 1, 2010, then the old insurance company would have denied payment on those claims because the old policy was canceled.

To correct this problem and get the claims processed as quickly as possible by the new insurance company, please send both the original billing information and the Medicare EOB information that you have for any unpaid claims with dates of service on or after October 1, 2010 directly to the new insurance company. Following is the contact information for that insurance company.

>> Claims Dept.
> Mucho Moolah Ins. Co.
> P.O. Box XXX
> Marble Hill, MO 63764.

Thank you for your cooperation.

>> Sincerely,

>> Mary Q. Contrary
> 1000 Bubba Blvd.
> Unit AOK
> Valparaiso, IN 46385

* * * * * * * *

LETTER TYPED FOR CLIENT TO CORRECT HOSPITAL BILLING RECORDS

February 17, 2011

Patient Accounts
Happy Healthy Hospital
1234 Bloody Blvd.
Indianapolis, IN 462XX

Dear Representative,

    I believe that your records are incorrect. This letter should help you to correct them. Accompanying this letter are copies of two pages to help you pinpoint the problem.

    Your records claim that I have an insurance policy with Blue Moon Ins. Co. I have not had a policy with that company for almost 20 years. I have a Medicare supplement policy with Red Moon Insurance Company which is based in Atlanta.

    My insurance agency's administrator Mr. Woodrow Wilcox helped me to phone your office to discuss the problem. Your representative claimed that the inaccurate information came from Medicare. Mr. Wilcox helped me to phone Medicare and Medicare's representative said that Medicare's records showed that I have a policy with Red Moon Insurance Company. So, the inaccurate information in your records did not come from Medicare.

    Please, correct your records so that there will be no problem in the future with your firm getting paid by the proper party if I use your services again.

Sincerely,

Donald T. Rump
987 Wilcox Way
Griffith, IN 46319

* * * * * * * *

LETTER TYPED FOR CLIENT TO SEND TO MEDICARE

March 1, 2011

MEDICARE
[Addressed to a service center.]

Re:
Hurting Wife Smith
2222 Suffering Street
Highland, IN 46322

Re: Your letter to Hurting Wife Smith dated January 25, 2011

Dear Representative,

This letter is on behalf of my wife.

In your letter to her dated January 25, 2011, your office stated that she would receive $84 around February 2, 2011 for the reasons that were stated in that letter.

It is now March 1, 2011 and NONE OF THE MONEY PROMISED HAS BEEN RECEIVED.

But, the money that you promised to take from my wife's social security check HAS BEEN TAKEN FROM HER ON THE DATES THAT YOUR LETTER PROMISED.

Every time I call to talk to someone at Social Security, the representative tells me to talk to my insurance agent. Well, I did. No one at the insurance agent's office has anything to do with causing or solving this problem that Social Security and Medicare created for my wife.

I want my wife to be treated fairly by Social Security and Medicare. But, so far, that hasn't happened. Please, get on the problem and fix it.

Sincerely,

Helpful Husband Smith
2222 Suffering Street
Highland, IN 46322

LETTER TO HOSPITAL
RE: MEDICARE SKEWED NUMBERS

February 24, 2011

Patient Accounts
Saint Cashius Medical Center
P. O. Box XXXX
Hayden, IN 47245

Dear Representative,

I sent to my insurance agent's office a bill from your firm for their review. The dates of service on the bill are 07/30/2010 to 07/31/2010 with a balance due of $1,539.94.

They contacted my insurance company to learn what it knew of this bill. The insurance company reported that Medicare sent to it a claim for those dates which totaled just over two thousand dollars – not the $29,001.79 of total original charges on the bill that you sent to me.

To correct this error of Medicare and get the entire bill processed as quickly as possible, please send both the original billing information and the Medicare EOB information that you have regarding these claims directly to my insurance company. Here is the contact information that you need for that.

Claims Dept.
Sympathetic Insurance Company (SICO)
P. O. Box XXXX
Pigeon Forge, TN 37863

Thank you for your cooperation in this matter.

Sincerely,

Arzhuke Wah Shukran
1908 Delpha Drive
Greentown, IN 46936

* * * * * * * *

LETTER TO HOSPITAL RE: $480 BILL

March 9, 2011

Patient Accounts
Payusnow Hospital
P. O. Box XXXXX
Chicago, IL XXXXX

Dear Representative,

I sent to my insurance agent's office a bill from your firm for their review. The bill is for DATE OF SERVICE 11-11-2010 with a balance of $480.00.

They checked with my Medigap insurance company about this claim. Your bill's figures and the insurance company's EOB from Medicare DO NOT MATCH.

According to the insurance company, Medicare did not disallow anything on this bill. Medicare approved the bill at $1,671.75 and paid $1,164.06. The insurance company paid your firm $507.69 with check number XXXXXXX on December 28, 2010. That is more than the $480 balance sought on your bill to me.

Your bill to me is dated 01-11-2011. So, it is possible that the payment from the insurance company and your bill to me crossed in the mail. Please, review your records on this account. If the bill has been satisfied, please, send a new statement to me which shows that the balance is paid. If the bill has not been paid or if there is any other problem with the figures reported by my insurance company, please, contact the insurance company directly to discuss the matter and resolve any problems or errors. Here is the contact information that you need to do that.

        Med. Supp. Claims Dept.
        Luvtopay Life Ins. Co.
        P. O. Box XXXX
        Clearwater, FL 33757

Thank you for your cooperation in this matter.

Sincerely,

Sally Sufferin Succotash
1234 Eugene Avenue
Griffith, IN 46319

* * * * * * * *

LETTER TO ADVISE OF BILLING ERRORS

March 11, 2011

Patient Accounts
Wabash Moonlight Medical Clinic
1811 Tippecanoe Terrace
West Lafayette, IN 47906

Dear Representative,

When I got an unexpected bill from your firm, I was all shook up!

I visited my insurance agent's office and asked them to review documents that I brought there. The documents were bills from your firm and Explanation of Benefits statements from my insurance company.

Together, we made phone calls to my insurance company and Medicare to review the documents – including your firm's bills to me.

Based on that research, my insurance agent's administrator believes that there is a billing problem at your firm. In fact, we were advised by a Medicare claims specialist to inform your firm that the claims from your firm which are being denied are being denied because of "not enough information being provided to show the medical necessity of the procedure or service." The same Medicare claims specialist told us to request that your firm contact the Medicare provider line for more information on the reasons for the denials.

Also, some of the notations on the insurance company's explanation of benefits forms tipped the insurance agency administrator that the problem originated with your billing department. Here are quotes of some of the statements from the insurance company EOB statements to me.

"The amount not payable includes the difference between the charge amount and the Medicare allowed amount, which cannot be balance billed by the provider."

"Charge exceeds fee schedule/maximum allowable or contracted/legislated fee arrangement."

We have requested DUPLICATE MEDICARE SUMMARY NOTICE statements for all denied claims in the past 15 months.

Please, review the denied claims from your firm, contact Medicare about the reasons for the denials, and re-file the claims with augmented notes to support the medical need for the services rendered.

Thank you for your cooperation in this matter.

Sincerely,

Elvis P. Elvis
1935 Songandance Drive
Myrtle Beach, SC 29588

* * * * * * * *

LETTER TO HOSPITAL TO REVIEW AND CORRECT BILL

Patient Accounts
Mississippi Mud Medical, P.C.
999 Flooded Parkway
Dubuque, IA 52002

Dear Representative,

I brought to my insurance agent's office a copy of a bill from your firm and a copy of the related Medicare Summary Notice and asked why Medicare and my Medicare supplement insurance policy did not pay the entire bill from your firm. The bill is for services rendered on 08/16/2011 and has an unpaid balance of $202.

They reviewed the papers and found that the Medicare Summary Notice footnote "a." to the claim stated, "The information provided does not support the need for this service or item."

It seems that the bill did not get paid because your firm did not supply the required information to demonstrate the medical need for the service. Please, review this claim and augment the notations with the claim to demonstrate the medical need for the service. Then, re-file the claim with Medicare. That may resolve all the issues and get the bill paid.

Thank you for your cooperation to make sure that I am billed fairly and without overcharges that might be caused by errors.

                    Sincerely,

                    Mark Twang
                    555 Recording Stars Road
                    Murfreesboro, TN 37127

****

LETTER TO HOSPITAL TO CORRECT BILL TO ZERO

                    December 22, 2011

Patient Accounts
Serving Sickies Medical Clinic
888 Serving Sickies Street
Otis, IN 46391

Dear Representative,

I sent a bill from your firm to my insurance agent's office for review. The date of service is 10/07/2011 with an unpaid balance of $1,132.

They contacted my insurance company. It reported that it paid this bill to your firm with check number XXXXXXX for $1,132 which was sent to your firm on 11/14/2011.

Medicare reported the name of the medical service provider for this claim as "Serving Sickies Medical Research Foundation". That is the name on the check that your firm cashed. It is confusing and unfair to senior citizens and insurance companies for your firm to file the claim under one name with Medicare and send a bill in a different name to the senior citizen.

Please, correct this billing error promptly and send a new statement to me which shows the balance owed as zero. After all, you did cash the check and you have been paid. Don't make a senior citizen suffer financially because someone at your firm "goofed" a bill. If you have any concern or dispute on this matter, please contact my insurance company directly regarding the cashed check and the payment according to Medicare regulations. Here is the contact information.

Claims Dept., Sioux Everybody Life Ins. Co.
P.O. Box XXXX, Sioux City, IA 51111

Thank you for your attention to this matter.

Sincerely,

Felicia Feelinworse
777 Gamblers Way
Gary, IN 46404

* * * * * * * *

LETTER FOR CLIENT TO SEND TO MEDICAL SERVICE PROVIDER

December 16, 2011

Patient Accounts
Over the Hill Medical Services
666 Inyourpockets Parkway
Branson, MO 656XX

Dear Representative,

I was surprised by bills from your firm which totaled $888 for four charges of $222 on various dates because I have both Medicare and an excellent Medicare supplement insurance policy.

I presented your bills to the senior medical bill case worker at my insurance agent's office. He reviewed the bills and requested copies of my Medicare Summary Notice forms which related to these bills. I believe that he found the problems with these bills. YOUR FIRM IS ATTEMPTING TO DOUBLE BILL ME FOR SERVICES WHEN YOU WERE ALREADY PAID. Let me explain.

You received Medicare EOB notices that have exactly the same information that I describe in this letter as being on the Medicare Summary Notice form that I received which is dated November 14, 2011 with file number XXXXXXXX with nine pages.

The three dates of claims for $222 four times are 8/19/11, 9/16/11, and 9/27/11. On these dates and for these charges, you billed me twice. For the first such charge on each date, Medicare ruled that the approved amount for the claim was $30.80, that Medicare paid your firm $24.64, and that I or my insurance company could be charged the balance of $6.16. On the second charge of each day which you tried to double bill me, the Medicare footnotes on my MSN form give one or both of two statements which are as follows:

- "Payment is included in another service received on the same day."
- "This is a duplicate of a charge already submitted."

Here is a list of the Medicare claim numbers that I know relate to this matter. There may be more.

XX-XXXXX-XXX-XXX
XX-XXXXX-XXX-XXX
XX-XXXXX-XXX-XXX
XX-XXXXX-XXX-XXX

Check your records and change your records to show that the balance owed by me is zero. If you have any dispute with the accuracy of this letter, send both the original billing information and the Medicare EOB information on each unpaid claim directly to my insurance company at:

Claims, Healthy Odds Ins. Co., P. O. Box XXX, Reno, NV 89501.

Sincerely,

Luwanna Lewinski Lincoln
123 Fire Station Avenue
Lansing, IL 60438

* * * * * * * *

LETTER TO CREDITOR AND COLLECTION LAW FIRM

January 3, 2012

Patient Accounts
Maybe a Medical Service Provider, LLC
11 Satan Street
Calumet City, IL 60409

Cc: Maybe A Medical Service Provider, LLC, HQ, 666 Devil Drive, Chicago, IL 60666

Cc: Hittem, Hurtem, and Shakemdown, P.C.

Dear Representative,

    I took a bill from your firm and a collection letter from your law firm to my insurance agent's office and asked them to review it with me.
    The bill from your firm gives neither a date of service nor a place of service. I am a senior citizen with Medicare as the primary insurer and We Really Care Insurance Company as the secondary insurer. We contacted We Really Care Insurance and it received no crossover claim from

Medicare regarding your firm nor for any service to me with a balance due of $310.

If you did not file this claim with Medicare, then do so. If you did file this claim with Medicare, then send both the original billing information and the Medicare EOB information directly to my insurance company for processing. Also, recall the bill from the collection law firm. It is not the fault of a senior citizen when either your firm or Medicare fails to send the claim to the insurance company. It is unfair to "ding" the credit of a senior citizen in such a circumstance. So, don't harm me that way!

Here is the contact information for my insurance company.

Claims Dept., We Really Care Ins. Co.
P. O. Box XXX, Seymour, IN 47274

Thank you for your cooperation.

Sincerely,

Oxhalah Moonlight Gatorspotter
P. O. Box XXXXX
Seminole, FL 33772

* * * * * * * *

LETTER ABOUT NO RECORD OF CLAIM

July 11, 2012

Patient Accounts
Clogged Pipes Plumbing and Medical Service, P.C.
P. O. Box XXXX
Black Oak, IN 46406

Dear Representative,

I brought a bill from your office to my insurance agent's office for a review.

Solving Medicare Problem$

    The senior medical bill case worker at my insurance agent's office examined the bill and compared it to the Medicare Summary Notice forms that I provided. Your claim was not on those forms. We phoned my insurance company to learn what it knew of this claim. It reported that it had no record of such a claim.

    I was told that if the client did not receive the claim report on a Medicare Summary Notice and the insurance company did not receive the claim report on a Medicare EOB form, then it is highly likely that either your firm never filed the claim with Medicare or Medicare goofed and did not forward the claim properly. I don't know what happened. I just don't want to be financially harmed because of a mistake by someone else. The man who helped me said that this probably is Medicare's fault and not the fault of your office.

    To fix this problem in the quickest way possible, please send both the original billing information and the Medicare EOB information about any unpaid claim directly to my insurance company for processing. Here is the contact information that you need.

                           Claims Department
                           Mister Quick Pay Insurance Company
                           555 Just Kidding Lane
                           Yazoo City, MS 39194

Thank you for your cooperation.

                           Sincerely,

                           Cathy De Dancin Clogger
                           101 Donut Hole Drive
                           Burns Harbor, IN 46304

CHAPTER EIGHT

MORE ARTICLES FOR GREATER UNDERSTANDING

THREE HOURS FOR ONE CLIENT

On September 22, 2011, I spent three hours helping one 83 year old woman to fix the medical bill problems that she had because Medicare messed up the claims. The elderly client is from Hammond, Indiana.

Much of the time was spent on the phone with medical offices and insurance claims departments to get the bill facts. The client did not have the medical bills, Medicare Summary Notice forms, and insurance company Explanation of Benefits forms in order. In fact, most of what I just mentioned was missing.

Medicare failed to deliver essential claims information to our client's old and new insurance companies for multiple claims during three different years. I had to write and send six letters to various medical firms to get matters resolved. I am confident that my work will result in our client's medical bills being paid according to her Medicare supplement insurance policy.

One bill was from a collection firm. For that problem, I wrote to both the hospital and the collection firm. I informed the hospital that Medicare never sent the claim to the client's insurance company. I asked the hospital to send certain vital claim information directly to the insurance company for processing of the claim and to recall the bill from the collection firm. I told the collection firm about the Medicare caused problem, advised them what was being done to fix the problem, and asked them to cease all collection efforts.

(Written in September 2011)

* * * * * * * *

ASK FOR HELP WITH VA-MEDICARE PROBLEMS

On July 27, 2011, a veteran and his wife visited my office and asked for help with a Veterans Administration & Medicare problem. The client is a senior citizen from Merrillville, Indiana.

Several years ago, I wrote an article about VA-Medicare problems. That article was widely published and distributed. The problem then was more serious and widespread. I made waves with the VA. I kept phoning the next higher person in the chain of command until I finally got someone in Washington, D.C. to agree to take calls and letters from our veteran clients who were having problems.

Since then, I have heard of few problems in the VA-Medicare medical billing arena. But, the client who visited me on that day told me that he had the same problem over a year ago and that it took him a year to get the problem corrected. So, he came to our office to get me to help with the new medical bill problem.

Fixing a problem among the Veterans Administration, the Medicare system, and an insurance company to make sure that the VA, Medicare, and the Medicare supplement insurance policy all pay the correct amount on a medical bill is an ordeal.

Then, I realized an easier and better way to deal with this problem. Ask a congressman or senator to help. Members of Congress and the U.S. Senate can get the cooperation of the VA and Medicare systems to correct a medical billing error faster than I or our client can. Also, it is important for U.S. Congressmen and U.S. Senators to know that there are medical billing problems for veterans in dealing with the VA and Medicare. If we, the people, don't tell the elected representatives that there are problems, they never will realize that there are problems because the bureaucrats in Washington won't admit it and tell them about problems.

The help that an insurance agent or agency can give such a veteran is to write an introductory letter to the elected official and his staff to specifically describe the problem that the veteran faces in the billing problem between the VA and Medicare. This will show respect for the time of the staff member who is assigned to help with the matter. That is what I did.

This is a more practical way to get the help that is needed to resolve a medical bill problem that involves two federal government agencies. I strongly suggest this action be taken in similar situations to give veterans the help that they need when they need it.

(Written in July 2011)

* * * * * * * *

SAVED HIGHLAND WOMAN OVER $2500

Two mistakes occurred. A client made a mistake and her insurance company made a mistake. The result was that a medical bill for over $2,500 was complicating our client's life. The client is an elderly woman from Highland, Indiana.

The client's mistake was miswriting the insurance company's name on a check. The insurance company decided that it could not cash the check as it was written. The insurance company's mistake was waiting a week before trying to contact the woman about the problem with the check. In that time, the client's policy lapsed for non-payment.

The elderly woman thought that she had insurance. So, she had some tests done on her doctor's advice. But, because she did not have an active Medicare supplement insurance policy, she was responsible for the 20% of the bill that Medicare did not cover. That amounted to over $2500.

Wow! Was she surprised when she got that bill. She and her husband phoned the insurance company, but they could not get the policy reinstated. Then, they visited me.

I listened to them and copied the information that they had. I phoned the insurance company and learned what its records showed. I found the key problems and wrote a letter to the insurance company which highlighted the errors that its employees had made. I pointed to the insurance company's own records to cite the errors and then told them that cancelling the policy was not fair to our elderly client under the facts of the matter.

Executives at the insurance company agreed. The policy was reinstated. The claim was paid.

(Written in September 2011)

* * * * * * * *

WORKING WITH AN ANGRY DAUGHTER

On the morning of June 29, 2011, I received a fax which was a copy of a payment demand letter from a bill collection law firm regarding a $1,100 bill to one of our clients. On the fax was a handwritten note which said, "Supplemental insurance is supposed to pay for this!" The bill was for a client who is an elderly woman from Hobart, Indiana.

The note was not signed. I tracked and contacted the sender by calling the firm from which the fax was sent. I learned that the fax was sent by the angry daughter of one of our clients. I got an earful from the angry daughter. It was a lovely way to start my day.

I know that people are busy. I know that children of the elderly who care for their parents have a busy schedule. But, why not alert your parent's insurance agency of a medical bill problem before it is sent to a collection attorney? The sooner an insurance agent or agency learns of a medical bill problem, the easier it will be to work to fix the problem. Doesn't that just make more sense than waiting until a payment demand letter is sent from a law office?

I worked to resolve the matter. I phoned the insurance company and confirmed my suspicion that Medicare never sent the claim to our client's insurance company.

I wrote a letter to the hospital and the collection lawyer about the $1,100 claim. My work for the client resolved the bill and collection matter. I know that the Medicare system fails many senior citizens with its terrible mistakes. But, it would have been easier for me to help with this bill problem if the bill had been sent to me before it went to a collection attorney or a collection agency.

I am able to help most of our clients with billing problems. The three matters in which I usually can't help a client are (1) when the bill problem is given to me too late and the deadlines for changing matters have passed, (2) when a client has signed an *Advance Beneficiary Notice* which obligates the patient to pay the bill even if Medicare refuses to pay anything, and (3) when the bill problem is caused by a policy of Medicare and the federal government which is designed to push more costs onto senior citizens in order to help the federal government to save money.

(Written in June 2011)

* * * * * * * *

SURPRISE MEDICARE RULING COSTS SENIOR

I was surprised by a Medicare ruling on a bill to a senior citizen client. In over eight years of helping senior citizens with Medicare related medical bills, I never encountered a Medicare ruling like the one that is described in this article. The ruling stuck our client with a $162 bill that neither she nor our agency expected. The woman who was hurt by the Medicare ruling is from Valparaiso, Indiana.

Following is part of the letter that I sent to our client which explains the matter to her. Everyone can learn from it. The Medicare ruling is that a person can be a patient in a hospital, but get outpatient services. That ruling seems strange to me. How can a person be both an "inpatient" and an "outpatient" at the same time? If all the services given to our client were "inpatient", she would owe nothing because of her Medicare supplement insurance policy that she bought with the help of this insurance agency. But, when Medicare ruled that some of the services were "outpatient", the formula changed and our client was stuck with a bill.

I never heard of such a ruling before now. It seems to me that this is another example of how the federal government is changing rules and regulations of Medicare to "push" more costs onto senior citizens in order to save the federal government money. Below here is an excerpt from the letter that I sent to the client who is being stuck with a $162 bill.

Dear Client,

I phoned your insurance company to learn what it knew of the $162 charge. The insurance company informed me that Medicare ruled that you owe the $162. Although you were an inpatient from January 1 to January 31, 2011, Medicare ruled that some services that you received from January 3 to January 7 constituted outpatient services. Outpatient services are covered by Medicare Part B and inpatient services are covered by Medicare Part A.

By federal law, there are annual deductibles for both Medicare Part A and Medicare Part B. Medicare supplement insurance policies vary in that some do and some do not cover the deductibles for Medicare Part A and Medicare Part B. In 2011, the annual deductible for Medicare Part B is $162. This means that you, the patient, are responsible for the first $162 of Medicare approved Part B charges in 2011. Medicare ruled that the first $162 of Medicare Part B services that you received while in the hospital was your annual deductible and that you are responsible to pay this.

I do not know why Medicare ruled this way. To learn the details, find and read the Medicare Summary Notice that you received from the federal government which describes how Medicare made this determination and ruling. If you can't understand it, you may call this office to schedule a time when I could review it with you and maybe make a phone call to Medicare together if there are any questions.

Thank you for allowing us to help you with your insurance needs.

(Written in July 2011)

* * * * * * * *

ACCIDENTS AND MEDICARE CLAIMS

On November 30, 2011, I helped a senior citizen couple with some Medicare medical bill problems. The couple was from Merrillville, Indiana.

I spent two hours with them in the afternoon. I reviewed the papers that they brought to our office and made phone calls with them.

They had several problems. But, I learned of a new type of problem which could affect other senior citizens, too.

When a senior citizen is in a car accident, Medicare becomes a secondary insurance after other insurance. When a senior citizen who was in a car accident gets medical treatment after the accident, and the medical treatment is not related to the car accident, the medical service provider must make that clear on the claim form. With an electronic filing, there is a place to mark to tell Medicare this. With a paper claim form, the information must be written.

If there is no notation on a claim form to Medicare that the medical treatment is not related to the car accident, the claim form will default to denote that it is related to the car accident. In such a case, Medicare will deny the claim.

So, it is important for every senior citizen who is injured by a car accident to remind every medical service provider to mark on the claim form to Medicare that the service is not related to the car accident when that is the case. This will save the senior citizen some grief and money.

(Written in December 2011)

* * * * * * *

UNREALISTIC RULES AND REGULATIONS

A client of this insurance agency visited me with paperwork about a medical bill problem that was being caused by Medicare. The senior citizen client was from Highland, Indiana.

The man got a Medicare supplement insurance policy with a high deductible from his former employer for free. Although it had a high deductible for hospital, doctor office, and clinic expenses, it had great prescription medicine coverage.

The man bought a regular Medicare supplement policy, also. The regular Medicare supplement policy had a lower deductible than the free policy provided by a former employer.

This caused confusion at Medicare and among the insurance companies of the client.

Because the free policy provided by an employer was the first one registered with Medicare, it took a senior position among the insurance companies even though that was not what the client wanted.

With the client present, I phoned Medicare for advice. Medicare does not have a workable system to accommodate such a situation. This exposes the unrealistic rules, regulations, and guidelines of Medicare. What the client wanted was quite practical. It took advantage of the wonderful prescription drug coverage offered in his retirement by a former employer. And, it solved the high deductible problem of the free policy.

Medicare advised for our client to write a letter to the insurance company of the free policy from the employer and request that it cancel the Medicare information crossover connection, but not the policy itself. If that does not work as desired, we will phone Medicare with our client again.

The help that we gave to our client was provided free of charge by this insurance agency.

(Written in September 2010)

* * * * * * * *

NICE THANK YOU NOTE

On August 10, 2011, I received a thank you note from a client whom I had helped with a medical bill problem. The client lives two counties away from where I work. This insurance agency has many clients who are not within fifteen miles of our office because our reputation has spread. Following here is a portion of the letter.

Dear Woody,

A note to thank you for being so helpful in responding so quickly to help me in my need to straighten out my situation with [the medical service provider].

Before contacting you, I had talked to the person in patient accounts but without much response.

Thank you for stepping in to get this resolved. Sometimes, it just takes a little help from a friend at our Senior Care Insurance Services to right the situation.

I appreciated the kind words. I hope that my articles inspire some other people to start helping senior citizens with this national problem of mistakes in medical billing that is caused by the federal Medicare system.

(Written in August 2011)

* * * * * * * *

NICE APOLOGY FROM HOSPITAL

On August 3, 2011, I received a very nice letter of apology from the patient finance manager of a hospital that had overbilled one of our clients by almost $600.

When I reviewed the bill that was sent to our client, I found certain questionable entries. I wrote a polite letter to the hospital telling them what I thought might be in error on the bill and asked the hospital billing department to review the bill again.

When the hospital reviewed our client's bill, it agreed with me that the bill contained errors. The bill was corrected and recalculated. Our client owes nothing. My work saved the client $578.75. I thanked the hospital manager for her cooperation.

The Medicare system is far from perfect. In every system, technical errors and human errors happen. I just strive to protect our clients from financial harm when those errors occur.

(Written in August 2011)

* * * * * * * *

SAVED CROWN POINT WOMAN $1100

On October 25, 2011, I received a pleasant surprise telephone call from a local hospital. The work that I had done to help an elderly client finally resulted in a good resolution. The client that I helped is from Crown Point, Indiana.

In early September, the client visited this office and showed me papers that related to an unpaid bill of $1,100. I checked on matters and then wrote a letter for our client to sign. Then, I mailed the letter with documentation for the client.

The letter was sent to a local hospital. The letter did not get to an appropriate person. Our client got another bill for the $1,100. So, we sent the letter and materials with another cover letter to a different party at the hospital. After receiving the second letter, the hospital took action and sent the essential information about the bill directly to the insurance company as the letters requested. When the insurance company got the information that it needed to legally process the claim, it sent a check for $1,100 to the hospital. Our client owes nothing.

The problem was that Medicare failed to send the essential information to the insurance company. Without the information, the insurance company was unaware that our client had been treated at the hospital. Also, without all the required information, the insurance company could not legally process and pay the claim.

This problem was not the fault of our client, the hospital, the insurance company, or our insurance agency. Medicare caused this problem. Medicare made a mistake. Medicare makes mistakes like this often. I wish that more people would help senior citizens to correct the mistakes of Medicare and help senior citizens to save money.

(Written in October 2011)

* * * * * * * *

THREE BILLS IN ONE MONTH

Three different times in one month a client came to me for help with Medicare related medical bill problems. The client is a senior citizen from Hobart, Indiana.

On December 5, I helped him with a bill for an unpaid balance of $4,909.54. On December 9, I helped him with a bill for an unpaid balance of $13.23. On December 27, I helped him with a bill with an unpaid balance of $375.87. That adds to $5,298.64.

In each case, I researched the problem and wrote a letter to get the problem corrected. The amounts were small, medium, and large. It doesn't matter. He was our client. We know that the Medicare system is not perfect. When mistakes happen and problems occur, we do our best to protect our senior citizen clients from financial harm.

The service that I gave to this client was FREE OF CHARGE. Does your insurance agent or agency deliver the same high standard of service to the senior citizens that you know? If not, why not?

(Written in December 2011)

* * * * * * * *

HOSPITAL DOUBLE BILLED CLIENT

On Wednesday, July 27, 2011, a client phoned a message to me to complain that a bill was not paid. I returned the call and had the client fax the bill to me. The client is an elderly woman from northwest Indiana.

The bill was for physical therapy from a hospital in northwest Indiana. The unpaid balance was $132. The woman used this insurance agency to obtain a very good Medicare supplement insurance policy from a very good insurance company. So, a bill for an unpaid balance would be very unusual with these facts.

I phoned the insurance company to learn what it knew of the bill. The insurance company already paid the bill. The check that the insurance company sent cleared the bank over a month before the demand for payment of the unpaid balance bill was sent to our client.

To help our client, I wrote a polite but firm letter to the hospital and cited the date that the check was cashed and the number of the check from the insurance company. When the hospital gets the letter, I expect that the records will be corrected to show that the bill is paid and that our client owes nothing.

(Written in July 2011)

* * * * * * * *

BILL INFO DID NOT MATCH

An elderly lady got a bill from a hospital for $620.75. She sent the bill to me and asked why she got a bill. She is a client of this insurance agency. She is from Highland, Indiana.

The client sent only the bill. She did not send a copy of the Medicare Summary Notice form from the federal government and she did not send a copy of the EXPLANATION OF BENEFITS from her insurance company. These items are other pieces of the puzzle when I investigate a Medicare related medical bill problem.

I contacted the client's insurance company. It got different information from Medicare than what the hospital sent in the bill to the client. In other words, what the hospital claimed was owed did not match with what Medicare told the insurance company. To help our client resolve the problem, I wrote a letter to the hospital. Following are a few paragraphs of that letter.

***

Your firm sent a bill to our client with an unpaid balance. She sent that bill to us and asked why she got a bill. She has a [very good] Medicare supplement insurance policy with a very good company.

The bill is for dates of service 6/17 through 6/30 in 2011. The bill states that the unpaid balance is $620.75.

The insurance company said that the report it got from Medicare showed nothing was denied by Medicare and that the final balance of the bill was $456.84. The insurance company sent to your firm a check for $456.84 on July 18.

Please, contact the claims department of the client's insurance company to review this bill and make any corrections needed. Our senior citizen client should not be penalized financially because someone in the system made a mistake. Here is the contact info you need.

***

The service that I gave to this client was FREE OF CHARGE.

(Written in July 2011)

* * * * * * * *

SAVED HIGHLAND WOMAN $345

An elderly woman sent bills to our office and asked why the bills were not paid by Medicare and her Medicare supplement insurance policy. The client is from Highland, Indiana.

I reviewed the bills and phoned the client's insurance company to ask questions about the unpaid bills. The insurance company had no claims regarding this client for the entire year. That means that MEDICARE FAILED TO SEND ANY CLAIMS TO THE INSURANCE COMPANY for the entire first half of 2011.

To help our client, I sent a letter to the medical service provider and explained this. I requested that the patient accounts manager send certain essential information about the unpaid claims directly to the client's insurance company for processing.

The fact that Medicare failed to send the claims to the insurance company is not our client's fault, nor the medical firm's fault, nor the insurance company's fault. It is Medicare's fault.

When the medical firm sends the information that I requested, I am confident that the claims will be paid by the insurance company according to the terms of the policy. This will save our client $345. If no one had helped her to fix this billing problem that was caused by the federal Medicare system, she would have been hounded by collectors to pay this debt which she really did not owe.

The help that I gave this client was provided FREE OF CHARGE. The owners and managers of this insurance agency really do care about our senior citizen clients. They pay me to help our senior citizen clients with Medicare related medical bill problems. It keeps me busy. Does your insurance agent or agency give the same high level of service to senior citizens? If not, why not?

(Written in July 2011)

* * * * * * * *

SAVED CEDAR LAKE MAN OVER $500

On July 19, 2011, an elderly client phoned me and complained about a bill from a local hospital not getting paid. I told him that it would be better if I could see the bill and any other related papers rather than have him describe things over the phone to me. He made an appointment with me for the next day. The senior citizen is from Cedar Lake, Indiana.

At the appointment, he showed me bills from a local hospital and some papers from his insurance company. I reviewed the papers with him and wrote a letter to the hospital to fix the problems that I found.

The hospital was billing our client for an unpaid balance of $507.45. But, according to the insurance company's report to the client, it paid that $507.45 with a check on May 18, 2011 – two months before the client phoned and met with me.

I found another discrepancy in the papers. The hospital claimed that the total original bill was over $5,000. But, Medicare sent the claim to the insurance company with a total original charge that was substantially under $5,000. In other words, either Medicare or the insurance company did not get accurate and correct information and that was messing up the claim, too.

My letter to the hospital for our client explained the problems that I had found when I compared the bill to the insurance company's information. On behalf of our client, I requested that the hospital do certain things and contact the client's insurance company to review and correct the billing problems. I told the hospital that our senior citizen client should not be penalized financially because someone in the system made a mistake. I believe that what I did will result in the $507.45 being paid and credited to zero the balance for our client. So, I saved the client over $500.

(Written in July 2011)

* * * * * * * *

BEE STING AND BILL STING

An elderly woman who is a client of this insurance agency phoned me for help with a bill. I recommended that she visit our office and bring any papers that related to her Medicare supplement medical bill problem. The client is from Highland, Indiana.

I reviewed the papers and made several phone calls to the hospital that was billing her, to the insurance company, and to Medicare with the client present so that she could give her permission to talk to me about her medical bill problem.

The medical bill "problem" became the medical bill "problems" during the phone calls. There were two basic problems with the bill from the hospital. In each case, it was a matter of innocent human error.

The first problem was that our client's insurance company did pay on the bill. It paid exactly what Medicare reported that it should pay. But, Medicare gave the insurance company several addresses for the hospital. The check was not sent to the correct address of the patient accounts department. While I held the phone, the insurance company representative confirmed to me that the check was sent but never cashed. I helped the insurance company to get the correct address for payments. The old, uncashed check will be voided and a new check will be sent to the hospital.

The second problem with the bill was that someone at the hospital miscoded the medical service as an allergy treatment and Medicare did not realize that the service to the woman was for serious swelling from a bee sting in an emergency room service. Medicare will pay for that service if it is described and coded correctly. The hospital billing department person with whom I spoke got my point right away and agreed that the bill should be corrected and resubmitted to Medicare. She promised to have that done.

So, I was able to eliminate a medical bill to our client by getting the facts corrected so that Medicare and our client's Medicare supplement insurance policy would pay all of the bill.

After I finished with the client, she said to me, "I never could have done what you did. I don't know the system as well as you know it."

My service to this client to eliminate the bill was without any charge. Does your insurance agent or agency give the same high standard of service? If not, why not?

(Written in June 2011)

* * * * * * * *

MEDICARE MAKING "PIDDLY" WORK

On August 12, 2011, I got a phone message from a medical service provider in Lake County, Indiana. When I returned the call, I got a surprising bit of information about how the federal Medicare bureaucrats have been forcing medical service providers and insurance companies to do lots of time consuming, money consuming "piddly" work. In other words, the federal government has been driving up costs to doctors, hospitals, and insurance companies under the current leadership.

Since January 2011, Medicare has been reprocessing claims for services rendered from January 2010 through May 2010. It seems that Medicare officials were "wishy washy" and "flip-flopping" on percentages for payments to medical service providers in 2010. So, Medicare decided to re-do all the claims in that period.

This forced medical service providers and insurance companies to re-do their books for all the claims for that period.

I discovered this by writing a letter to a medical service provider regarding a small bill for $2.89. I thought that the small amount was for interest during the period from when the client got the medical service to the time that the doctor's office got paid. Nope. It was the new unpaid balance after Medicare recalculated the claim.

Before that Medicare recalculation, the insurance company relied on the first claim calculation to pay what it owed. So, before the Medicare recalculation, our client's bill was paid in full by Medicare and the Medicare supplemental insurance company.

Medicare's recalculation of claims program is causing an enormous amount of expensive and time consuming work for insurance companies, hospitals, doctors, and laboratories. In all that recalculating, mistakes are bound to happen. In one instance, the person who brought this to my attention got a phone call from an irate patient. The patient was upset because Medicare applied $162 of a claim to his annual deductible for 2010 Medicare Part B claims when in fact his prior claims had already met the annual deductible. In other words, MEDICARE'S GOOF CAUSED THE PATIENT TO OWE ANOTHER $162.

The patient was angry because he thought that the doctor's office caused the extra bill. Nope! It was the anointed and infallible public servants at Medicare who caused the problem and the bill. So, don't be upset with your doctor, hospital, laboratory, or insurance company if you get a newly recalculated bill for medical services that you received sometime from January through May in 2010. Blame it on Uncle Screw-Up, er, uh, I mean Uncle Sam and the Obama administration's management team at Medicare.

(Written in August 2011)

* * * * * * * *

MEDICARE LOST 2 OF 3 CLAIMS

On May 2, 2012, I helped a client who is from Munster, Indiana. He brought to our office a bill from a medical service provider with an unpaid balance.

I phoned the client's Medicare supplement insurance company to learn what it knew of the unpaid bill. The insurance company reported that Medicare sent only one of the three claims to it. So, Medicare failed to send two of the three claims that were filed.

The three claims were for original billed amounts of $245, $225, and $75. The insurance company got the claim for $245 and paid its portion of the claim. But, it did not get the other two claims from Medicare. You can't blame an insurance company for not paying a claim that Medicare never sent to it.

To help our client, I sent a friendly letter to the medical service provider and explained what the insurance company had reported to me. I requested that the medical service provider send certain essential information about the unpaid claims directly to our client's insurance company for processing. When that is done, I am confident that the insurance company will pay the claims according to the terms of the insurance policy that our client bought.

The help that I provided to this senior citizen client was FREE OF CHARGE. When one of our senior citizen clients has a problem, we do our best to help resolve the problem. Does your insurance agency give this high level of service to its senior citizen clients? If not, why not?

(Written in June 2012)

* * * * * * * *

MEDICARE REFUSED BREAST AND PELVIC EXAMS

On July 16, 2012, I helped an elderly woman from Gary, Indiana. She wanted to know why her doctor's office sent her a bill for $199 for breast and pelvic exams despite the fact that she had both Medicare and an excellent Medicare supplement insurance policy.

She showed me a bill but no Medicare Summary Notice. So, I could not compare those items. I phoned her insurance company to learn what it knew of the bill. It reported that Medicare refused to pay anything for the breast and pelvic exams. If Medicare won't pay for something, then the Medicare supplement insurance will not pay either because Medicare disallowed it.

To help our client, I wrote a letter to the doctor's office and asked them to review their records on the filing of the claim with Medicare. If a mistake was made in the filing of the claim, that could be corrected and the claim could be re-filed. But, if Medicare is refusing to pay on the bill due to a government policy change that is designed to save the federal government money and push medical costs onto senior citizens, then our client will be stuck with a bill that she did not expect.

I don't yet know the outcome of this matter. But, I do know that I have done everything that I could do to help the client to avoid financial harm from the Medicare system. Does your insurance agency give its senior citizen clients this high level of assistance? If not, why not?

(Written in July 2012)

* * * * * * *

PRIVATE ENTERPRISE MOVES FASTER

On May 23, 2012, I received a medical bill from a senior citizen client who lives in Hammond, Indiana. The bill had an unpaid balance and our client wanted to know why since she had both Medicare and a Medicare supplement insurance policy through the insurance agency where I work.

I contacted the client's insurance company to learn what it knew of the claim. The bill was for services rendered on April 1, 2011. The insurance company did not get the claim from Medicare until May 7, 2012. That is over a year after the medical services were rendered.

The insurance company made and sent a check to pay the bill on May 7, 2012 which is the same day that the insurance company got the bill. The check was cashed by the medical service provider on May 17, 2012. So, our client's bill was paid and she owed nothing.

After a doctor, hospital, or other medical service provider renders service to a senior citizen who has Medicare coverage, the medical service provider has a little more than a year to file the claim with Medicare. Maybe that is what happened in this case. But, the other possibility is that the claim was temporarily lost or misplaced by Medicare. In either case, the medical service provider had to wait more than a year to be paid and our client had to wait more than a year to get her bill paid. But, the privately owned and run insurance company paid the bill on the same day that it got the bill from Medicare.

Private enterprise moves faster.

(Written in May 2012)

* * * * * * * *

MEDICARE RECORDS UPDATE SLOW

On Friday, May 25, 2012, a client visited this insurance agency with a Medicare related medical bill problem. An agent introduced me to the woman. She asked if I am the fellow who writes the articles that appear in many local newspapers.

"Yep!" I responded. She was delighted. She told me that she felt better just knowing that I was going to help her. The client is from Merrillville, Indiana.

I reviewed the papers that she brought and asked her some questions. She had just retired and started on Medicare recently. I suspected that Medicare had not updated her records to show that she was on Medicare now and no longer on another insurance plan with her former employer. So, together, we phoned Medicare to learn what its records said. I was right.

The Medicare representative reported that although the client started on Medicare on February 1, 2012, that information was not entered in her file until March 29, 2012. All the claims for service for dates of service from February 1 to March 29 had been processed incorrectly by Medicare because of this slow update of our client's records.

The miscalculation of all the claims that our client had during that period threatened to cost our client almost a thousand dollars. To help our client, I wrote a polite letter to all the doctors and clinics that had given her service during the period of Medicare's bad records. I explained what happened and that it was the fault of Medicare and not the fault of our senior citizen client. I asked every doctor and clinic to re-file their claims now that the Medicare records were correct so that a proper figuring of the claims could be made.

When the claims are re-filed, the problem will be corrected so that our client's medical bill problem will go away. The help that I gave this client was FREE OF CHARGE.

(Written in June 2012)

* * * * * * * *

HELPING AN UPSET VETERAN

A veteran came to our office in Merrillville, Indiana. He was upset about a bill from the Veterans Administration. The bill for over $300 was for visits to a doctor at a VA Clinic. He wanted to know why Medicare and his Medicare supplement policy were not paying the bill.

When the veteran got the services, the VA thought that he had a low enough income to qualify for the medical services at no charge. But, in

2002, the law was changed so that veterans who have an income over certain levels set by the VA will be charged $15 for a visit to a general doctor and $50 for a visit to a specialist doctor at a VA clinic.

The VA checked with the I.R.S. about his income level. The VA determined that our client should have paid the $15 or $50 charge to visit a doctor at a VA clinic. It sent him the bill.

The VA does not bill Medicare. If Medicare does not get a claim and rule favorably on the claim, then neither Medicare nor a Medicare supplement insurance policy will pay the bill. If the veteran client had visited private doctors instead of visiting the VA clinic, both Medicare and his Medicare supplement insurance would have paid on the bills.

Our client was upset with us about the unpaid bill. But, we don't write the rules about how the VA and Medicare should treat his health care bills. We have a good record of helping our clients when there are mistakes in the Medicare system. But, we can't change the results of a government policy. There is a limit to what we can do.

To help our veteran client, I typed some letters which questioned the bill and had him sign each letter. There were grounds to question the bill. I discussed the matter with our most experienced agent and thought of some ways to help the client. I phoned the client's insurance company to discuss the VA – Medicare – insurance claims problem and got some other ideas to help the client.

A few weeks later, the client was excited when he returned to our office to show me a letter that he received from the Veterans Administration. They admitted that they made a big mistake by not sending the revised bill through the normal claims process with a certain government contractor that connected VA claims with Medicare and supplement insurance companies.

In this case, federal government rules and regulations prevented me from helping our client to get the entire bill paid. But, I was able to help the client by nudging the VA to follow its own rules which will get part of the bill to our client paid. The point is that I helped the client to get the best possible resolution under the circumstances.

(Written in May 2012)

* * * * * * * *

PAID BILL SENT TO COLLECTION

A client of this insurance agency got a bill from a collection agency for the balance of a hospital bill and sent it to me on May 14, 2012. The client lives in a rural area about 80 miles from our main office in Merrillville, Indiana. He wanted to know why he got a bill when he had both Medicare and an excellent Medicare supplement insurance policy.

I contacted his insurance company to learn what it knew of the bill with the unpaid balance.

"We paid that bill almost a year ago!" the insurance company representative reported to me. The balance of the bill from the hospital for $181.95 was paid to the hospital by check on March 28, 2011 and the check was cashed on May 24, 2011. But, the hospital sent the bill to a collection agency which sent a demand for payment letter to our client that was dated April 30, 2012. The hospital had cashed the check almost a year before the collection letter was sent.

Medicare did not cause this problem. The hospital's accounts receivable system caused it. The hospital in a rural county let another hospital in another county handle its billing and collections. The larger hospital in another county contracted with a billing and collection service in Chicago to take payments. The insurance company check was sent to the Indiana hospital in care of the address of the billing and collection service in Chicago. The insurance company sent the payment there because that was the address for payment that Medicare reported to the insurance company.

The check was cashed, but the Indiana hospital gave the bill to a collection service in Tennessee. I wrote a letter to both of the Indiana hospitals, the billing service in Chicago, and the collection agency in Tennessee. I cited the number of the check that was sent and cashed, the dates of the issuing and cashing of the check, and other facts of the matter. I requested that if any of them had falsely reported our client's account as delinquent that they recall and remove the false bad credit information.

All the help that I gave to this client was FREE OF CHARGE.

(Written in May 2012)

* * * * * * * *

CHINESE AMERICAN CLIENT HAD A QUESTION

On July 11, 2012, a Chinese American gentleman who bought a Medicare supplement policy through our agency brought some bills to our office and asked me why the bills had unpaid balances.

"I thought that Medicare and my Medicare supplement insurance policy would pay everything. Why are there balances owed on these bills?" the client asked me.

"I don't know, sir. Have a seat and let me do some checking," I answered.

With copies of the bills in front of me, I phoned our client's insurance company to learn what it knew about the bills. There were two bills from two different medical service providers with a total of three dates of service on the two bills.

For date of service January 30, 2012, the insurance company received incomplete information about the claim from Medicare. The insurance company could not legally pay the claim without the complete information. It wrote letters requesting the complete information but had received nothing yet.

For date of service April 19, 2012, Medicare sent two claims to the insurance company, but those claims did not have the same figures or add to the same totals as the figures on the hospital bill.

For date of service May 3, 2012, Medicare reported the total original charge on the claim as $387 and not the $646 total that the hospital bill showed.

I helped the client by writing letters to both medical service providers to explain the bill problems and ask them to send their bill information directly to the client's insurance company. My letters should save the client almost $330.

In my letters about these medical bills, I stated that the problem was not caused by our client and I don't want our senior citizen client to pay extra money because someone else made a mistake. In this case, I believe that Medicare made the mistakes and caused the problems.

The help that I gave to our client was FREE OF CHARGE. Does your insurance agency give the same high level of service to senior citizen clients? If not, why not?

(Written in July 2012)

* * * * * * * *

MEDICARE 18 MONTHS PAST DUE

On July 12, 2012, an insurance agent in our office delivered information to me about a Medicare related medical bill of one of our clients who is over 90 years old. The client is a friend of the agent as well as a client. He asked me to work to fix the problem right away and I did.

The bill was from a hospital in another county for services rendered on January 9 through January 14 of 2011. The bill was for $1,132. I got the bill a year and a half after it was made.

I checked with our client's Medicare supplement insurance company. Medicare never sent the claim to the insurance company. Eighteen months had passed. The hospital or its collection firm was getting ready to sue our elderly client. The hospital did not cause this problem. The insurance company did not cause this problem. Our insurance agency did not cause this problem. Our senior citizen client did not cause this problem. MEDICARE CAUSED THE PROBLEM BY FAILING TO DELIVER CLAIMS INFORMATION TO THE INSURANCE COMPANY FOR EIGHTEEN MONTHS.

The bill represented the Medicare Part A annual deductible which was covered by the client's policy. The insurance company was ready and willing to pay the bill. It just needed Medicare to deliver the claims information so that the insurance company could pay the bill.

This situation is another example of why I believe that government health care programs are not as reliable as many people believe.

The help that I gave to this client was FREE OF CHARGE. Everyone at this insurance agency really cares about our senior citizen clients and we do our best to serve them well. Does your insurance agency give this high level of service to its senior citizen clients? If not, why not?

(Written in July 2012)

* * * * * * * *

ANOTHER TYPICAL DAY

On Wednesday, June 20, 2012, I had a rather typical day. The Medicare system is not perfect. I help senior citizen clients of this insurance agency to correct Medicare related medical bill problems every day. The help that I give is free of charge because it is to clients of the insurance agency that employs me.

For clients from Schererville, I wrote a letter to their doctor to alert his office to some errors that they were making which were "gumming" the Medicare claims process for our clients.

For a client from Crown Point who is handicapped, I made phone calls with her to eliminate $1,987.90 of unpaid medical bill problems and worries. She told me that she would sleep better after visiting our office and getting my help.

For a client from Hobart who is handicapped, I made phone calls with her to her doctor's office and her insurance company to fix a Medicare related medical bill problem of $225.

For a client from Whiting, I phoned her and her insurance company to fix a bill problem of about $200.

Then, a client from East Chicago phoned me to complain about some Medicare related medical bills that were not getting paid. I told him that I can't guess at the problem over the phone. I need to see the bills and that I really want to review the bills with the client in the office. I invited the client from East Chicago to visit our office and bring the bills so that we could work on the problems together. He agreed to visit me in two days.

Does your insurance agent or agency care enough about senior citizen clients to go the extra distance and make the extra effort to help them with Medicare related medical bill problems without charge? If not, why not? Giving such help to senior citizen clients is all part of a typical day at Senior Care Insurance Services in northwest Indiana.

(Written in June 2012)

* * * * * * *

MEDICARE IS A COMPLICATED SYSTEM

On July 5, 2012, I returned a phone call to a business office of a hospital for one of our clients. I was surprised by the information that I got in the call.

For one of our clients, Medicare reprocessed the claim and took back some money that it had paid the hospital. Medicare changed its payment to the hospital from $10,000 to only $6,000. This changed all the calculations of how much was left on the bill for the hospital, the insurance company, and the patient who had bought the insurance through this agency.

The more parts that a machine has, the more likely that some part will malfunction and skew or stop the function of the machine. Medicare and Medicaid are complicated like that. When something goes wrong, the system does not work.

I really believe that the Medicare and Medicaid systems were not designed to help patients get needed medical attention. I believe that the systems were designed to enrich special interests who work for the government or for government industry contractors.

For almost a decade, I have helped senior citizens to save money by finding and correcting errors in medical bills that were caused by mistakes in the Medicare system. Also, I have worked as a consultant and editor for research regarding problems with the Medicaid system. These systems have and make problems. Under Obamacare, the rest of America will start to experience the flaws and frustrations which government control of health care causes.

(Written in July 2012)

CHAPTER NINE

SELF-ADMINISTERED DRUGS

THE "SELF-ADMINISTERED DRUG" PROBLEM EXPLAINED

In 2010, I was surprised by a new problem that was facing our senior citizen clients more and more. It was the problem of "self-administered drugs". I tried to help our clients with this problem, but it seemed like the "system" was stacked against the senior citizens. Then, I wrote a letter to two U.S. Senators and an article about it.

I did not know what the source of the problem was. I thought that if I wrote such a letter and article that some people in the federal government would realize that there is a problem with Medicare that is hurting senior citizens and would want to work to resolve it. I learned that it is more complex than that. I believe that I got these two senators interested in this cause, but that's about it. There is a lot of resistance from special interests that profit from keeping a government program just as it is even if it means harming senior citizens who are supposed to be helped by the government program.

While helping some of our senior citizen clients in late 2011, I had conversations with two different Medicare representatives on the phone. I questioned each of them about why our client in each case had stayed in a hospital overnight for surgery in the hospital but had been classified as an "outpatient" when the hospital filed a claim with Medicare. The "outpatient" classification caused the patients to be billed for "self-administered drugs" which would not be covered by Medicare Part B. Each representative told me that it was the doctor's notes to the hospital which controlled whether the patient would be classified as an "inpatient" or an "outpatient". From this, I thought that maybe if I helped the client write a letter to the doctor to ask that the doctor write a note to the hospital to classify the client as an "inpatient" that this might help the client and eliminate or reduce the bill for "self-administered drugs".

Then, the week of Christmas 2011 to New Year day 2012 was slower than usual for our office. The issue of "self-administered drugs" started to gnaw at me. Was there someone that I could call or something that I could find on the internet that could help me to help our clients and senior citizens on Medicare everywhere? I wondered. So, in between my other work, I started phoning and searching on the internet.

An acquaintance who works for a major insurance company in Indianapolis told me that she believed the problem of "self-administered drugs" causing big medicine bills for seniors on Medicare had been happening for only about three years (2009, 2010, and 2011). A supervisor in claims at a hospital system in Indiana told me that the problem has intensified in the last three years since Barrack Obama's Attorney General of the United States Eric Holder had been in office. She said that Eric Holder increased "RAC Audits" which check on how hospitals classify a patient. She said that the criteria for whether a patient is an "inpatient" or "outpatient" for Medicare purposes is set by Medicare (the federal government). She told me that doctors must use that criteria to advise a hospital whether a patient is to be considered "inpatient" or "outpatient". If the doctor and hospital don't follow the Medicare criteria rules, and a patient is admitted as an "inpatient" instead of an "outpatient" in violation of Medicare rules, then Medicare won't pay anything. *So, the source of the "inpatient" or "outpatient" rules and the source of the "self-administered drugs" problem which causes money problems for senior citizens when they go to a hospital is the federal government – not doctors, nor hospitals, nor insurance companies, nor insurance agents! Let's put the blame where it belongs.*

I am not a lobbyist. I am not a researcher at a "think tank" in Washington, D.C. I am not a congressman or senator. I don't have an unlimited supply of money and time to research every little detail of this problem. I'm just a guy who does his best to help senior citizens every day to fix problems that are caused by the Medicare system. In a sense, I am "where the rubber meets the road".

From my viewpoint, it seems that the federal Medicare system has too much "doublespeak". Politicians, lobbyists, bureaucrats, and government industry contractors claim to want to build a government system that helps senior citizens when in fact they really don't. They want to create a government system that brings more power and profit to themselves – especially the government industry contractors. What other explanation could there be for having rules about getting medicine while in a hospital that are so complicated that they discourage senior citizens from making an effort to file claims? That is what we have right now!

I challenge you to check the internet for official documents and other material about the Medicare system. I suggest that you start by finding and reading the federal government's document *Billing for Self-Administered Drugs Given in Outpatient Settings; Revised February 2011; CMS Product No. 11331-P (www.cms.gov/partnerships/dounloads/11331-P.pdf)*. Or, you could learn how convoluted the process is for a senior citizen to get some reimbursement for "self-administered drugs" by reading the federal government's explanation in the document *How Medicare Covers Self-Administered Drugs Given in Hospital Outpatient Settings; CMS Product No. 11333; Revised February 2011 (www.medicare.gov/Publications/Pubs/pdf/11333.pdf)*.

People who work with billing at hospitals and doctors' offices attend training in person or via the internet to help them to do their difficult jobs. On the internet, I found an article about such a training session in which a student asked a very intelligent question about if it were possible that a drug could be integral to service in the case of one patient but self-administered in the case of another patient. The expert's answer started with "It is unclear. It depends . . . ."

Politicians, lobbyists, and news media promoted Medicare Part D to the public as a way to help senior citizens with prescription medicine costs. But, the complex and time consuming system for getting help with the costs of prescription drugs while in a hospital actually harms senior citizens financially. To me, it does not seem fair to force a senior citizen who is recovering from a hospital stay, or the relatives of a deceased senior citizen, to confront a myriad of forms, rules, and regulations to get the federal Medicare system to help pay for prescription medicine.

The author George Orwell warned America about "doublespeak" in his book *1984*. The "doublespeak" in the federal Medicare program creates confusion, problems, and loss of money and time for both senior citizens and the people in hospitals, medical offices, insurance companies, and insurance agencies who serve the senior citizens. As far as I am concerned, Medicare is a mess!

If I were the Secretary of Health and Human Services, I would do everything possible to eliminate the "doublespeak" in the Medicare system and anywhere else that I could eliminate it. I don't give a "hoot" about the special interests that seem to have a "grip" on Medicare now. I just hate witnessing senior citizens getting hurt again and again by the Medicare system. I hope that whoever becomes the next Secretary of Health and Human Services will have my attitude and will take action to change things so that the Medicare system stops hurting senior citizens.

(Written in December 2011)

* * * * * * * *

THE PROBLEM OF "SELF-ADMINISTERED DRUGS"

I wrote the following letter to two U.S. Senators:

Senators Lugar and DeMint

Dear Senators,

I am writing to both of you about a problem with the current Medicare system.

I am writing to Senator Lugar because the cases involve people from Indiana.

I am writing to Senator DeMint because he has taken the lead in the Senate on many health care issues.

Here is the problem. This year, a growing number of our senior citizen clients who get prescription drugs in outpatient settings are charged for "self-administered drugs" and Medicare Part B does not cover the costs at all.

I contacted the Chicago office of CMS, the Medicare service office, and was told that a senior citizen in such a situation could file a claim for refund on Medicare claim form 1500 which could be obtained at doctor offices, pharmacies, or social security offices.

This recommended solution is impractical for a senior citizen who is injured, ill, or dying.

The Medicare Part D system is poorly designed for senior citizen outpatient visits which often involve "self-administered drugs" – which basically means that the patient can put a pill in the mouth.

Because of the present BAD situation, our office has a growing number of senior citizens who are being billed for "self-administered drugs".

$30.15 for "self-administered drugs" is being charged to a man from Lowell, Indiana.

$200.69 for "self-administered drugs" is being charged to a woman from Hobart, Indiana.

$755.18 for "self-administered drugs" is being charged to a man from Highland, Indiana.

The man from Highland was admitted to the hospital overnight but the hospital charged him as an outpatient. It seems that someone is "playing games" with the criteria for "inpatient" or "outpatient" status which affects the Medicare calculations and the figure for any balance owed by the patient or the patient's insurance company.

More cases are in our files with similar "self-administered drugs" problems. Please, do what you can to eliminate this problem for senior citizens all over America.

(Written in March 2010)

* * * * * * * *

HELP WITH "SELF-ADMINISTERED DRUGS"

Starting in 2010, some of this insurance agency's senior citizen clients on Medicare began having problems with "Self-Administered Drugs" causing them to receive big prescription drug bills after staying in a hospital.

With each client present after bringing such a bill problem to me, I would make phone calls to Medicare to get help for the client. But, each time, I got somewhat unclear and different information from the Medicare representative who answered the phone call. It seemed like each client and I were getting "the run around".

During the week between Christmas 2011 and New Year 2012, our office was less busy than usual. In between my other work, I started making phone calls and searching the internet for information that would help me to help our clients with the "self-administered drugs" problem.

The problem happens when a senior citizen on Medicare with a Medicare supplement insurance policy and a Medicare Part D plan is in a hospital overnight but classified as an outpatient. Most hospitals do not bill the client's Medicare Part D plan for the prescription medicine that the senior gets while in the hospital. Instead, the patient is billed for the medicine.

Whether or not the senior citizen can get some reimbursement from the Medicare Part D plan company is a complicated matter which involves filing a claim, presenting receipts or bills, and figuring the difference between the hospital charge, the Medicare Part D plan charge, the positioning of the medicine on a formulary list, and some other factors.

It seems that the best possible source of help for a senior citizen who gets a bill for "self-administered drugs" is to contact the State Health Insurance Assistance Program in the senior citizen's state of residence.

This insurance agency helps senior citizens with relatively simple medical bill problems. By "simple", I mean that most of the problems involve putting back together bits of information to help our client get a Medicare related medical bill problem resolved and save the client money. I have helped our senior citizen clients to save more than one million dollars by correcting errors that were caused by mistakes in the Medicare system. But, the "self-administered drugs" problem is one that seems intentionally caused by the federal government. By that I mean that it is caused by design, at least since 2009 when Obama took office and his appointed Attorney General Eric Holder increased something called "RAC audits" of hospitals.

What no Medicare personnel told me in past phone calls was that the federal government defines when a patient should be classified as "inpatient" or "outpatient". Both doctors and hospitals must abide by Medicare's definitions. When a senior citizen is classified as "outpatient" and gets prescription medicine while in the hospital, the "self-administered drugs" bill is incurred.

Unfortunately, the process to help the senior citizen get some reimbursement from a Medicare Part D prescription plan is too complicated and time consuming for this agency to be able to offer help to our clients on this problem. The only way that we can help is to direct the senior citizen to the State Health Insurance Assistance Program. Those people get paid with tax money to help. How much help they can provide is something that I don't know.

I believe that the federal government intentionally made the reimbursement process complex and time consuming in order to discourage senior citizens from trying to get some reimbursement. In the past, the federal government "stacked" laws against Native American Indians, African Americans, and women. Now, it is "stacking" laws against senior citizens.

(Written in January 2012)

CHAPTER TEN

FUTURE PROBLEMS FROM "OBAMACARE"

The main purpose of this book is to introduce the reader to the work of helping senior citizens to save money by correcting problems and medical bill errors caused by mistakes in the Medicare system. It is the work that I have done for over nine years. But, I care about other things, also.

If you were standing at a street corner and saw another person about to step into the street into the path of an oncoming vehicle, you would be a very uncaring person if you did not do something to warn or stop the person who was about to step into the street. You might shout. You might grab the person's arm and attempt to pull the person from danger. But, if you did nothing, wouldn't others be correct to view you as a very uncaring person? I believe so.

Likewise, I have done my best to warn America about the dangerous step toward "Obamacare". If I did nothing and said nothing to protect Americans from this bad and dangerous law, I would be a very uncaring person. So, whether you agree or disagree with me, realize that my motive is to warn people, protect people, and avoid danger and problems for people.

I have written many articles against and regarding "Obamacare". But, I have included only eight of those articles in this book. If you read these articles and like them, you can read more of my articles about "Obamacare" at various publishing websites and my website www.woodrowwilcox.com. If you do not like these articles, then reading them has not cost you much time or effort. Accept my articles as a warning which you may choose to disregard. Everyone can learn something by reading these eight articles.

The new law that has become known as "OBAMACARE" has already started to cause problems for senior citizens. It will make more problems in the future if the law is not repealed or substantially modified.

The law transferred half a trillion dollars of anticipated future Medicare benefits from senior citizens to spend that money on other people and other things. That is like mugging and robbing every current and future senior citizen in America.

One of the first things that happened was that retirees of major corporations such as John Deere, Caterpillar, and others lost great prescription drug benefits that often had been negotiated under labor union contracts. This forced the retirees to spend millions of dollars more on prescription drugs that they did not anticipate.

The "Obamacare" law contained over 2,000 pages and did not get the public scrutiny that it deserved.

Obama and his allies in Congress who pushed for the new health care reform law complained that health care was being "rationed". They forgot to mention that much of the "rationing" was being caused by rules and policies of the federal health care systems that already exist. It seems that the "Obamacare" solution to lowering health care costs is simply to start to deny health care to senior citizens in order to save money for the federal government. If the federal government takes over all health care, everyone will experience the same kinds of problems that senior citizens now have with Medicare – the federal health care system for seniors.

The "Obamacare" law does contain language which is like "medical death panels". I interviewed a doctor from Indianapolis who went through the House Energy and Commerce Committee version of the bill and wrote an extensive and precise criticism of the bill in a letter to Senator Evan Bayh. I posted the doctor's letter and my video interview of him on the internet. His name is Dr. Stephen Frasier.

Medicare rules will be changed and more Medicare "double talk" will be written into regulation to gradually transfer more and more health care costs onto senior citizens.

The "Obamacare" law hurt children and all taxpayers, also. Be prepared for these things.

I care about and fight for senior citizens too much to say nothing against "Obamacare" in this book. In my view, the "Obamacare" law is the most anti-senior citizen federal law that was ever passed and signed. Obama, Reid, Pelosi, and their allies in Congress should be ashamed of themselves for hurting seniors with that law. Why didn't they take the time to refine and modify their ideas and words to make a health care reform law that would not target and harm senior citizens?

* * * * * * * *

MEDICARE MAKING PROBLEMS FOR BOTH DOCTORS AND PATIENTS

Editor-in-Chief Michael Cohn of *Accounting Today* (accountingtoday.com) wrote the article "Medicare Problems Only Grow Worse" for the edition of September 22, 2010. The article is available on the internet. It gives another view of the problems with Medicare under the Obama administration and the new health care reform law known as "Obamacare".

Doctors are not required to be part of Medicare. So, when doctors start to drop their connection to Medicare, won't that cause senior citizens some difficulty to find a doctor who accepts Medicare? That might be the case in the future. Here is what Michael Cohn wrote in the first paragraph of the article in *Accounting Today*.

> Doctors have been opting out of the Medicare system at an alarming rate lately as the system goes through a tumultuous year, leaving some accountants' clients in a bind when they suddenly cannot get their medical bills paid. [This refers to getting Medicare to pay the bills.]

In another part of the article, Cohn states that doctor offices "are having a hard time keeping up with the rapid changes in Medicare. The system is on its fourth physician fee schedule of the year, thanks to all the uncertainty and changes brought by the health care reform bill."

For years, I have been writing articles that expose the flaws in the Medicare system for senior citizens. For years, I have been helping senior citizens to get Medicare caused medical bill problems corrected. The system is far from perfect for doctors, too.

I appreciated the article by Michael Cohn in *Accounting Today* and would encourage people to find that article on the internet and read it. It is good to gain a perspective of the problem from another party's view.

(Written in January 2011)

* * * * * * * *

EYE DOCTORS COMPLAIN ABOUT MEDICARE

A client of this insurance agency sent a bill to me and asked me to check on why her insurance company had not paid on the bill. The client is a woman from Lowell, Indiana.

I checked with the client's insurance company. Medicare never sent the claim information to it.

So, I wrote a nice letter to the eye doctors' clinic to explain that there was a problem. I asked the doctors to send certain essential information on the claim directly to the client's insurance company so that the claim could be processed. I was surprised by the answer that I got.

The billing person at the eye doctors' office phoned me to tell me that she had phoned Medicare on several occasions. The eye doctors' office had sent the claim to Medicare in October 2009. But, at each of the several phone calls that the billing person made to Medicare, Medicare personnel claimed that Medicare was having technical problems with its computers and that the claim should be processed in two weeks. That is the "promise" that Medicare gave to the eye doctors' clinic every time the billing person phoned Medicare for the last eight months. And, according to Medicare personnel, the technical problem existed for some time prior to October 2009.

The billing person at the eye doctors' clinic was pleasant toward me and our agency's client, but very upset with Medicare. She assured me that our client would receive monthly statements until Medicare processed and paid the claim, but that the eye doctors' clinic would neither tarnish our client's credit nor try to force her to pay anything until after Medicare and her insurance company had processed the claim.

I really enjoyed this phone call from the billing person at the eye doctors' clinic. It was so nice to hear the voice of another person who is just as frustrated as I am with the federal government's Medicare system.

Don't forget: A larger federal government health care system will mean that more people will be able to experience the frustrating service of the federal government bureaucracy.

(Written in June 2010)

* * * * * * * *

FEDERAL MEDICARE BUREAUCRATS REFUSED TO PAY BILL

The federal Medicare system refused to pay for a senior citizen's pelvic and breast exams and pap smear.

A client of this insurance agency brought this to my attention. The client is from Munster, Indiana.

Her doctor wanted her to get these tests done. But, Medicare rules and regulations dictate when a senior citizen can and can't have these tests and expect Medicare to cover them.

In the case with our client from Munster, she needed the medical tests at a time that the federal Medicare system would not allow. So, she must pay the bill for these tests because the federal government's Medicare system won't.

If Obama and his allies in Congress create a new federal system of health care modeled on the Medicare system, then everyone in America can expect federal rules and regulations to dictate when they can or can't get medical services.

(Written in July 2009)

* * * * * * *

MEDICARE REFUSED TO PAY FOR X-RAY OF LOWELL MAN

On January 11, 2011, a client couple visited our office from Lowell, Indiana. They came for my help regarding an unpaid bill for an x-ray which was taken prior to surgery and as a precondition for surgery.

The man needed a knee replacement. The doctor would not perform the surgery until the man got a chest x-ray. Surgery is a shock on the human body. The doctor wanted to make sure that the patient was in reasonably good health to take the stress of surgery.

On June 1, 2010, the man from Lowell went to a medical clinic for the x-ray to satisfy the surgeon's requirement. The medical clinic protected itself by having the man sign an Advance Beneficiary Notice waiver. By signing the waiver, the senior citizen agreed to pay for the x-ray even if Medicare refused to pay for it. The medical clinic suspected from its past experiences that Medicare might refuse to pay for the x-ray. The medical clinic was right.

Medicare refused to pay anything for the x-ray of the man prior to his surgery. That left the senior citizen on Medicare with an unexpected $150 bill. In the Medicare Summary Notice, Medicare ruled that "The information provided does not support the need for this service or item." So, Medicare ruled that the chest x-ray required by the doctor as a precondition to surgery was not medically necessary.

If Medicare disallows a medical service charge, neither Medicare nor the Medicare supplement insurance company will pay for the claim. That is what happened in this case. The doctor believed that the x-ray was needed to avoid any complications from surgery. The patient thought that the x-ray was needed. Medicare disagreed.

Both the medical clinic and the patient appealed the negative ruling by Medicare. The patient's doctor provided a letter giving the reasons that the x-ray was medically necessary to prevent medical complications for the patient. Medicare stood by its decision to deny coverage of the x-ray prior to the man's surgery.

In the *Explanation of Decision* of the negative appeal ruling, Medicare stated, "We reviewed the facts presented in your case. . . . After reviewing this data it has been decided the diagnosis for this service is not one that meets coverage guidelines. . . . The service you received is deemed a routine or non-covered service. Medicare does not cover services provided for this type of care."

In the book "1984", author George Orwell warned of government leaders and bureaucrats adopting something he called "DOUBLESPEAK". That means that when politicians or bureaucrats say something, the average person ascribes one meaning to the words, but the politician or bureaucrat ascribes a different or twisted meaning to the words.

That is what is happening with Medicare and the federal health care system now. Expect more "doublespeak" from politicians and bureaucrats that will deny more and more Medicare benefits to senior citizens. The reason is that some politicians don't want to spend money on old, sick people when they could spend that same money on other people and things that they favor.

The "Obamacare" law took half a trillion dollars of future Medicare benefits away from senior citizens in order to spend it on other things and other people. What senior citizens and their doctors believe is medically necessary is being ruled as "routine or non-covered service" by politicians and bureaucrats who use "doublespeak" to hurt America's senior citizens. Expect more of this in the future. In fact, in my eight years of helping senior citizens with Medicare medical bill problems, I have noticed that this journey to such "doublespeak" has accelerated since Obama took office and especially since "Obamacare" became law.

(Written in January 2011)

* * * * * * * *

A PAINFUL BEGINNING FOR HEALTH CARE REFORM

On September 23, 2010, the initial parts of the health care reform law took effect. Just before that date, tens of thousands of children around America lost their health insurance because of stupid and irresponsible wording in the new health care reform law.

Two companies – Wellpoint and CoventryOne – cancelled the health insurance policies of thousands of children in California, Colorado, Missouri, and Ohio. Other companies did the same throughout the nation.

The law forced an unreasonable decision and deadline on health insurance companies that had covered children with pre-existing conditions. The federal law forced insurance companies to make a decision by September 22 and they did. Because of some stupidly written portions of that law, thousands of children who needed health insurance and had it have lost it.

How did this happen? Why did this happen? It happened because supporters of the health care reform bill rushed the bill and blocked any chance for serious examination and debate on every section of the bill. That prevented citizens from learning about the bill and instructing their elected representatives on how to vote. Without the debate and refinement of the bill, a bill which had provisions that were stupidly and irresponsibly written was passed. Because this bad law was passed thousands of sick children have no health insurance now even though they did have it before this law took effect.

There are all kinds of problems with the health care reform law. There are parts that don't even have anything to do with health care. One part of the law allows the hiring of a few thousand more I.R.S. agents. Another part of the law imposes new rules on the filing of 1099 Forms with the I.R.S. by small businesses. What does that have to do with health care reform? Nothing! "Health care reform" was used as a "cover" to push through new laws that benefited special interests groups that were represented by highly paid lobbyists that Obama, Reid, Pelosi, and their allies liked. Follow the money!

But, when I and others criticized the obvious flaws in the health care reform bill, the supporters of that bill called us all kinds of names. Many supporters of the health care reform law simply opened their mouths widely to scream hateful things and closed their eyes so that they would not have to see the problems with the proposed law that other people saw. That was an act of bigotry by those supporters of the health care reform law. They had their minds made up and they did not want to be confused by the facts.

Here's a painful fact. The new health care reform law caused tens of thousands of sick children to lose their health insurance because the law was written, pushed, and passed with stupid and irresponsible wording. If your senator or congressman voted for it, then your senator or congressman bears some responsibility for causing pain and problems for thousands of children who lost their health care insurance because of that bad law.

(Written in September 2010)

* * * * * * * *

"OBAMACARE" TV NEWS INTERVIEW

On January 18, 2011, I got a phone call from a reporter from WYIN-TV in Merrillville, Indiana. Renetta DuBose asked me if she could interview me about the possible repeal of "Obamacare". I agreed.

Renetta DuBose had interviewed me for the local news program in the fall of 2010 when the first parts of "Obamacare" came into effect. From that interview, I knew that my comments would be edited, but not in any negative way.

Here is an outline of what I said in the TV news interview when Miss DuBose asked me if "Obamacare" should be repealed.

- Yes, it should be repealed; it is a bad law that was badly written.
- "Obamacare" transferred half a trillion dollars in scheduled Medicare benefits for senior citizens and spent that money on other things and other people.
- "Obamacare" authorized the hiring of thousands of new I.R.S. agents. What does that have to do with health care reform?
- "Obamacare" destroyed great prescription drug benefits for labor union retirees at John Deere, Caterpillar, and other firms by punishing companies with more taxes if the companies helped their retirees with such benefits.
- "Obamacare" caused thousands of children who had health insurance to lose their health insurance in September 2010. This was because the law had some stupid and sloppy wording in it that threatened to punish insurance companies that had provided health insurance for the sick children affected.
- "Obamacare" did not get the public scrutiny that it should have received. Senator Harry Reid and House Speaker Nancy Pelosi pushed senators and congressmen to vote for the over 2,000 page bill without studying it or allowing time for the public to study it and comment on it. They worked to prevent any refinement and correction in the bill. So, it was like the first draft of a novel that gets published without any review and editing – it had a lot of really bad mistakes. The senators and congressmen who voted for it acted stupidly and irresponsibly. They never bothered to check

- the bill for anything that violated the Constitution or anyone's constitutional rights. That's a violation of their oath of office.
- "Obamacare" really did establish authority to start "death panel" reviews.
- "Obamacare" gave too much power to the Secretary of Health and Human Services to interpret the law and write any regulation imaginable.
- "Obamacare" gave the federal government a motive to start denying more and more procedures for seniors under Medicare in order to shift the costs of health care for seniors back onto the senior citizens. I gave examples of two clients of this insurance agency that I had helped. Medicare refused to pay for an x-ray related to a mammography for a woman from Valparaiso. Medicare refused to pay for an x-ray prior to surgery for a man from Lowell despite the fact that his doctor required the x-ray or would not do the surgery.
- "Obamacare", in my opinion, is the most anti-senior citizen law to ever be passed and signed into law. As far as I am concerned, actions speak louder than words. I believe that Obama, Reid, Pelosi, and their allies in Congress and elsewhere HATE SENIOR CITIZENS BECAUSE THEIR ACTIONS DEMONSTRATE A HATEFUL DISREGARD FOR SENIOR CITIZENS.
- "Obamacare" should be repealed so that a more sensible public discussion could be started. I am for health care reform, but "Obamacare" is not what we need. Let's pass a health care reform law that does not hurt senior citizens as "Obamacare" does.

(Written in January 2011)

* * * * * * * *

COUSIN IKE'S WARNING

When I was a baby, some of my relatives called me "Little Ike" because I looked a bit like President Dwight D. Eisenhower. It wasn't just because I was a bald baby and he was a bald President. He was my cousin. So, there really was a family resemblance.

My mother's father and Dwight D. Eisenhower were third cousins. They shared common great-great grandparents who were immigrants from Switzerland. I remember my grandfather telling me that they met only a few times in their lives at weddings and funerals. Both of them were in the U.S. Army in France during World War One.

I am a fifth cousin to David Eisenhower who is the grandson of Dwight Eisenhower and who married one of Richard Nixon's daughters. I never have met David Eisenhower. But, I hope to do so someday.

Some of my relatives repeatedly told me to pay attention to Cousin Ike. He was a smart and successful man. The advice given was that if I wanted to be a smart and successful man, I should pay attention to Cousin Ike. So, I did. Now, I'm urging everyone to pay attention to a warning from my Cousin Ike.

Many people know that in his last public address as president, Dwight D. Eisenhower warned Americans about the growing influence of a military-industrial complex.

"The potential for the disastrous rise of misplaced power exists and will persist," Eisenhower warned in the speech. But, he did not just warn about a military-industrial complex. He warned us about a dominating federal government aligned with various federal government contractors. *I nicknamed these "government industry contractors" or "GICs".*

"The prospect of domination of the nation's scholars by Federal employment, project allocations, and the power of money is ever present – and is gravely to be regarded," Eisenhower said. He continued, ". . . public policy could itself become the captive of a scientific-technological elite."

President Eisenhower was warning America about the growing influence of the federal government and those who make their living by contracting with the federal government – federal government contractors (including federal government employees.) Of course government industry contractors can negatively impact a state or community in a similar way, too.

Dwight Eisenhower was concerned that a powerful federal government and lobbyists for federal government contractors might push America to do things simply to increase federal government power and profit for federal government contractors. Eisenhower wanted America to take a balanced approach.

"We cannot mortgage the material assets of our grandchildren without risking the loss also of their political and spiritual heritage. We want democracy to survive for all generations to come, not to become the insolvent phantom of tomorrow," Dwight Eisenhower stated in the same speech. In another part of the speech, he said, "Good judgment seeks balance and progress; lack of it eventually finds imbalance and frustration."

How does President Eisenhower's last speech relate to today's problems with Medicare and related matters? I can answer that.

Big federal government contractors lobby for the federal government to have more money so that the federal government can give more money to big federal government contractors.

In the economic stimulus bill of 2009 that pumped almost a trillion dollars into the U.S. economy, General Electric (G.E.), a major federal government contractor, was given billions of dollars of economic stimulus money on top of the billions of dollars of contracts that it already got from the federal government. In the 2008 election cycle, G.E. owned or controlled the broadcast properties of NBC, CNBC, and MSNBC. Is it possible that a president and a congress that had just been elected with the help of news media coverage that was favorable to them simply returned a favor to a federal government contractor by giving away billions of taxpayer dollars to that federal government contractor? I believe that is very possible. I believe that is exactly what happened.

Until a few years ago, Westinghouse, another major federal government contractor, controlled CBS television and radio stations and networks. When Westinghouse controlled CBS, did it influence news presentations in order to promote a larger federal government and more taxes and regulations on America so that it could profit from more and larger government contracts? I believe that it did.

The Medicare system did not start until after big federal government contractors like Westinghouse and GE wanted to increase revenue from the use of satellites that these companies put in space. Federal government contractors made lots of money from military use of satellites. They wanted to make more money from the non-military use of satellites.

The Medicare system is built on the use of satellites, telephonic equipment, computers, and federal government contractors that perform various tasks in the Medicare system. All this costs billions of dollars and federal government contractors make billions of dollars because the Medicare system is designed as it is.

The real purpose of establishing the Medicare system was to make billions of dollars for federal government contractors. The publicly stated reason was to help senior citizens. An increase in the number of people who use a federal health care system would let federal government contractors make billions of dollars more in profit and increase the power and scope of the federal government. I believe that explains why anti-Obamacare advocates had such a difficult time getting their point of view in front of the public. Big government contractors who control a significant portion of America's licensed broadcast media stood to make billions of dollars if "Obamacare" were passed.

Here is my point. I don't believe that the current Medicare system is designed to help senior citizens. Also, I do not believe that the "Obamacare" law is designed to help all Americans with health care coverage. I believe that both systems were designed to put billions of dollars into the pockets of federal government contractors. I believe that a better Medicare system could be designed and that a more realistic health care reform law could be designed that would cost taxpayers less money, be more efficient, and waste less time and money if only we could get rid of the influence of federal government contractors who want to protect the billions of dollars that they gain from the system as it exists now.

I have great ideas for improving Medicare and America's health care system. But, I don't believe that I am the only one who has great ideas. In the public discussion about health care reform, President Obama, the Democrat leaders in the Congress, and the federal government contractors controlled media regularly ignored or marginalized the voices and concerns of many smart people.

We should repeal "Obamacare" and have a real discussion about health care reform. But, that can be done only if we first outlaw federal government contractors' control of the discussion by ownership of America's broadcasting interests. We can't have a productive and useful discussion on health care reform if big government contractors who control much of the broadcast media do everything to silence, slander, or ridicule anyone who has an idea that threatens their income from government contracts. I would like a law passed that forbids major federal government contractor companies, organizations, or other interested parties from owning or controlling significant interests in broadcast stations, networks, satellites, or other communication properties. The goal would be to "free up" much of the broadcast media so that more people and ideas could be heard in our national discussions.

I believe that in the past the federal government contractors that controlled major media outlets slanted the news, slandered or marginalized people and ideas that threatened their interests, and promoted with positive publicity the people and groups who stood for more federal government, more federal taxes, more federal regulations, and more money for federal government contractors.

(Written in October 2011)

* * * * * * * *

MY GRANDMA AND MY PROFESSOR

After I wrote the first draft of this book, I let my mother read it. She is good at proof reading. Her father, my grandfather, was an English, speech, and journalism teacher. He taught her well and he taught me well. But, it is difficult for most authors to proof read their own material.

After my mother read the first draft of this book, she told me something that I did not know. When Medicare was being debated in Congress, my maternal grandmother lobbied against it. She believed that Medicare would do more harm than good toward America's senior citizens. It would destroy the right of senior citizens to keep their personal health matters private. After all, if the federal government would review your bill, the federal government would know everything about your private health history. She saw this as an attack on every citizen's right to privacy from inquisitive government employees and others.

My grandmother believed that at some point, the Medicare system and the federal government would control health care over all senior citizens. Then, if the government decided that it cost too much to provide health care for a senior citizen, the senior citizen patient would be denied health care. The federal government would start making health care and life and death decisions that had always been reserved for a patient, the patient's doctor, and the patient's family. She foresaw the establishment of "federal death panels". She did not call it by that name. But, a rose by any other name is still a rose and a "death panel" by any other name is still a "death panel".

This talk with my mother triggered an important memory for me. In my first year of college, I attended a debate about Medicare because my science professor was the debater speaking against Medicare. I remember that he warned that the Medicare system would lead to higher and higher health care costs. The main reason for this is that Medicare would establish a new federal bureaucracy. This new bureaucracy would create rules, regulations, and forms which would be written in federal bureaucratese – not English. Doctors, hospitals, and other medical service providers would need to hire administrative people who could understand and follow the rules and respond to the bureaucracy when communication was needed. All this would drive up the costs of a patient to get medical help.

My experience in helping senior citizens with Medicare problems leads me to believe that both my grandma and my professor were correct.

(Written in October 2011)

CHAPTER ELEVEN

WRITING ARTICLES ABOUT SOLVING MEDICARE PROBLEMS

After you succeed in helping some senior citizens by solving Medicare problems, you may want to brag about it. Be careful. Don't disclose any sensitive information without the written consent of the senior citizen involved. Before you publish anything, seek and get professional advice to avoid problems. But, the senior citizen that you help might be nice enough to write a letter to the editor of your local newspaper to publicly thank you for your help in solving a Medicare medical bill problem. After such a thank you letter is published, expect more people to contact you to ask for help.

If you notice the articles that I write, you will see that I make my point without discussing anything sensitive. I pay attention to the rules and do my best to follow both the letter and the spirit of the law.

At some point, I began writing a paragraph to end each article which read something like this: The help that I gave this client was FREE OF CHARGE. The owners and managers of this insurance agency know that the Medicare system is not perfect. When mistakes happen, we do our best to protect our senior citizen clients from the financial harm that could result from those mistakes. Does your insurance agency give the same high level of service to senior citizen clients? If not, why not?

An ending paragraph like that helps people to realize that there is a difference in insurance agencies. An insurance agency or attorney or any business that gives added value service is appreciated by any consumer. If you help senior citizens with Medicare problems, you will gain business and build on your business reputation. If you help senior citizens and write good, concise articles that people appreciate, your business should grow even faster.

Remember my friend James Flack from Indianapolis? Remember his comment that he thought that I might be the only person in America who was helping senior citizens this way? Well, I don't know if I am the only person doing this work. There may be others. There may be many others. *But, I believe that I am the only one who has been helping seniors with Medicare medical bill problems and writing about it.*

There is something else about my articles and me which I would like you to know. I have been writing articles for a long, long time. I enjoy investigating, researching, and writing.

My maternal grandfather was an English, speech, drama, and journalism teacher who retired the year that I was born. In his retirement, his grandchildren became his last pupils and I was at the front of the class because I was the oldest grandchild. My grandfather founded my high school's newspaper – *The Panther Press* of Griffith High School in Griffith, Indiana. I believe that I got some writing genes from him.

In both years that I was in high school journalism and worked in the school news bureau, I won the "Outstanding Staffer of the Year" award. I was admitted to Quill and Scroll, an honor society for high school journalism students. A few times on a rotating basis, I was co-anchor of Calumet Area High School News on WCAE-TV from Lake Central High School in Saint John, Indiana.

In college, I studied journalism and was admitted to Sigma Delta Chi – The Society of Professional Journalists. I was earning a double major in journalism and political science (with an emphasis on political economics) when something happened. My grandfather was murdered.

This put an enormous emotional and financial strain on my family and me. A double major can take more classes and more money to complete. I decided to finish college earlier than anticipated. I graduated with a degree in political science while being short by one course for a degree in journalism.

Since then, finding work as a journalist or writer has been tough at times because I don't have the degree.

Maybe that is why I really have enjoyed helping seniors and writing about Medicare problems for over nine years.

My hope for this book is that it will inspire the formation of a team in every congregation of worship in America. I hope that each team will have at least one attorney, one insurance agent, one congregation leader, and one layman who want to work together to help senior citizens in their respective congregations and communities.

Maybe then, politicians and bureaucrats in Washington will become painfully aware that many, many Americans care very deeply about helping senior citizens and *SOLVING MEDICARE PROBLEMS.*

CHAPTER TWELVE

FINAL THOUGHTS

I enjoy watching demonstrations of fun and funny science and engineering.

Have you ever seen such a demonstration in which a simple task is performed by a long series of events?

I mean something like a machine that is started by an alarm clock which then signals this or that and a chain reaction of events to start to cook eggs or a pancake or make a toaster or coffee maker start to work.

Maybe you can think of a simple machine which performed well until it was changed into something more complicated. The more parts a machine has, the more chance there is that a part will malfunction and the machine will not work properly.

The same is true with health care. The more complicated and complex government interference makes the system, the more expensive it becomes and the more likely that something will malfunction and cause the system not to work properly.

When I was a young boy and got sick, sometimes a doctor would come to our home to treat me. Our home was on a small farm in Griffith, Indiana. Sometimes, my mother took me to a doctor's office in downtown Gary or Hammond.

My father was a mechanical engineer at Inland Steel Company in East Chicago, Indiana. My mother was a licensed music teacher but was staying at home with her children at the time. We were not rich or poor. On just my father's earnings, we could afford health care.

With the introduction of the federal government's programs of Medicare and Medicaid, federal rules, forms, procedures, and systems started. This complicated the health care system and increased costs for hospitals, doctors, laboratories, and insurance companies. Every time a new federal rule or procedure was introduced, medical service providers and insurance companies had to retrain personnel to comply with the new law, regulation, or procedure.

Government employees and government industry contractors benefited from more and more government money spent to keep the complicated health care system going.

Dramatic increases in health care costs were caused by government interference – not greed from doctors, hospitals, or insurance companies.

Medical service providers and insurance companies were forced to spend more time and money to comply with more and more government laws, regulations, and procedures in order to deliver health care to those who needed it. And the doctors, hospitals, laboratories, and insurance companies had to pass those costs onto the consumers of health care.

I believe that there are people in government who use government power to create new problems and then claim that to solve the new problems, more power should be given to those in government. Then, they repeat the process to make more problems and gain more power. It is a deceptive way to destroy freedom so gradually that few people notice it until it is too late to reverse the process and re-establish freedom from government dictatorial power.

Obamacare was designed to gain total control of Americans by controlling whether or not they get health care. It puts government officials in charge of deciding who, when, and whether a person who needs health care will get it.

Apart from the political considerations, Obamacare will usher a huge number of new regulations, rules, and procedures. This will create more chances of breakdowns and errors in the medical billing systems. And that will create a greater need for people to learn the system well enough to help people who are wrongfully charged bills that they can't understand and never should have received.

I have helped senior citizens to save money by correcting medical bill errors that were caused by mistakes in the Medicare system. With the start of Obamacare, millions more Americans will start to experience the flaws and frustrations which government managed health care causes. There will be a growing need for people who can help patients to deal with medical bill problems that are caused by the Obamacare government health care system.

Under Obamacare, the new health care system is not designed to help people who need medical help. It is designed to gain government control over people and enrich the special interest groups like government contractors and government employees who will get rich from the Obamacare government health care system.

I can design a better health care system. But, many people in government service and government contractor firms would oppose the system that I would design because they wouldn't be able to gain power and money with my design of a health care system.

I have heard that there are firms and organizations that offer formal training in how to resolve medical bill problems. I never had any formal training. I just learned as I helped clients of my friend's insurance agency. My views are not based on government or government contractor training. My views are based on experiencing the system "where the rubber meets the road".

I wrote this book to make the public aware of the need to help senior citizens with medical bill problems that are caused by flaws in one of the federal government's health care systems – Medicare. The federal Medicaid system causes problems, too. Now, the Obamacare federal government health care system will cause problems for everyone. Maybe you are one of the people who can help many other people to fix mistakes and problems caused by some part of the federal health care system. If so, I wish you well.